cooling conflict

A new approach to managing bullying and conflict in schools

To 'Tracey' and all the brave and generous students
who have wholeheartedly given us their trust and
shared their intelligence and creativity with us
and with each other throughout the life of the program.

cooling
conflict

A new approach to managing bullying and conflict in schools

JOHN O'TOOLE, BRUCE BURTON AND ANNA PLUNKETT

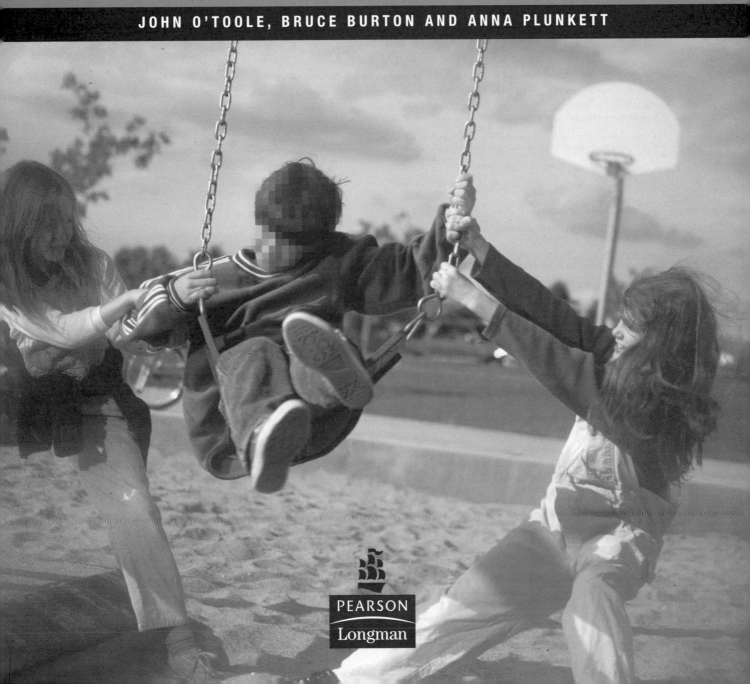

PEARSON
Longman

Pearson Education Australia
Unit 4, Level 2
14 Aquatic Drive
Frenchs Forest NSW 2086

www.pearsoned.com.au

Publisher: Diane Gee-Clough
Project Editors: Louise Burke and Carolyn Robson
Cover and internal design by designBITE
Cover image supplied by Getty Images
Typeset by Midland Typesetters, Maryborough, Vic.

Printed in Malaysia

1 2 3 4 5 09 08 07 06 05

National Library of Australia
Cataloguing-in-Publication Data

O'Toole, John.
Cooling conflict: a new approach to managing bullying and conflict in schools.

   Bibliography.
   ISBN 1 74091 121 0.

   1. Bullying in schools – Australia. 2. Bullying in schools – Australia – Prevention.
   3. Conflict management – Australia. 4. School improvement programs – Australia.
   5. Drama in education – Australia. 6. Peer counseling of students – Australia.
   I. Burton, Bruce, 1945– . II. Plunkett, Anna, 1976–. III. Title.

371.580994

An imprint of Pearson Education Australia
(a division of Pearson Australia Group Pty Ltd)

contents

preface

This book addresses a number of audiences – teachers, school administrators, parents, tertiary students and possibly some senior students, as well as all those people outside education with a concern and interest in the area of conflict and bullying in schools.

Three fundamental concepts inform the book:

○ The first is a recognition that conflict and bullying are among the most serious and intractable problems in virtually all school systems, from the multi-campus high school to the one-class community school . . . and not just among the students.
○ The second is that there is a universal desire to see something done about both conflict and bullying so that there can be better outcomes, particularly for the students.
○ Thirdly, that all previous attempts to solve the problem have had very limited success, if any, in the past 20 years.

The harsh reality is that there are no quick-fix solutions to the manifestations of conflict and bullying in schools. These can range from petty squabbles, ill-tempered schoolyard vendettas and older students standing over the new arrivals, to the systematic exclusion of those who exhibit difference, and the sustained victimisation of individual children. Some of the attempts to deal with conflict and bullying are indeed quick-fix, and both common sense and statistics show their results are as quickly forgotten. Others are the result of painstaking care over long periods, as schools endeavour to put conflict and bullying management plans in place.

Cooling Conflict seeks to give students themselves the tools to change the culture of their schools. The students gain cognitive understanding of conflict and bullying using a combination of drama and peer teaching within the curriculum in a whole-school context. The practical program outlined in the second part of this book has a number of very unusual and even radical features, some of which run quite counter to the thinking behind standard conflict management plans. All of the innovative features in the book are informed by a vision of student empowerment that is based on key principles of philosophy and pedagogy. These principles need to be understood before implementing the program. This is why Part One provides a thorough introduction to the eight years of practical experiment, exhaustive reading and action research that produced *Cooling Conflict*.

The full program cannot be achieved piecemeal, or in a slapdash fashion based on short-term contingency. It is possible to skip Part One and just follow the instructions in Part Two, using some of the drama in Chapters 6 and 7 and perhaps a bit of the peer teaching 'how-to'. Doing this may well help address some conflicts in some school settings, because drama techniques are now becoming quite an established part of anti-bullying and conflict management, and there are plenty of them in this book for teachers to work with. However, to truly establish a whole-school conflict and bullying management program which is genuinely empowering requires implementation of the whole *Cooling Conflict* program described here.

The book is designed as follows:

Part One: The program's principles

○ The Introduction briefly gives the background history of the program, providing the context and introducing the key principles.

○ Chapter 1 looks at the nature of conflict and bullying, providing the conceptual structure which the students themselves need to know in order to achieve the program's aim, which is their own *real* empowerment.

○ Chapter 2 explains the bases of the two key strategies that work in combination, when the context has been put properly in place, to achieve this student empowerment: *peer teaching* and *structured drama techniques*.

○ Chapter 3 provides examples of the student learning and empowerment provided by the program, from a wide range of schools with by now over 5,000 students.

Part 2: Implementing the program

○ Chapter 4 sets out exactly what is necessary for the program to operate in a school, or preferably, a group of schools – the infrastructure that will ensure it is not here today, gone tomorrow, like so many brave initiatives in this field.

○ Chapter 5 explains everything that teachers need to implement the program in their class-rooms, and explains how to operate the first of those key strategies – whole-class peer teaching.

○ Chapter 6 is a step-by-step guide to the other key strategy, an exciting and tightly structured form of classroom drama entitled 'enhanced forum theatre'.

○ Chapter 7 gives a further range of drama techniques that are useful ancillary teaching tools, either directly in the program or in extension and spin-off projects within the school and even the local community.

○ Appendix 1 gives a full glossary of the technical terms used, including the specialised terminologies of conflict and bullying management, of drama and of the program itself.

○ Appendix 2 provides some ready-made resources for using the program in the classroom.

○ Appendix 3 gives an extensive bibliography for further reading.

A note about references and readability

This book is intended for the general reader, the practitioner and the academic. The program is based on a formal and ongoing action research project, during which the copious literatures on conflict management, bullying, cultural conflict and cultural studies, drama education, arts education, constructivist educational theory and innovative pedagogies including peer teaching have been extensively consulted. Many of the insights from this literature have been transformed into the working principles and structures of this program, some immediately, some more distantly processed. To have detailed the research and cited all the references would have created a massive text unreadable to the lay audience. Accordingly, the only readings referenced in the text are those few that are quoted directly. Those readers seeking a more detailed understanding of the research that underlies the program and the literature that informed it are directed to the bibliography.

Key terms from the *Cooling Conflict* program and the specialised fields of conflict and bullying, drama and peer teaching appear in the glossary in Appendix 1. When first used, or where a clear definition may be useful, these terms are highlighted in the text using **bold** type.

acknowledgments

The authors would like to give admiring thanks to all the participating students, teachers, principals, school administrators, parents, education officers and consultants involved in *DRACON*, *Cooling Conflicts* and *Acting Against Bullying* since their inception.

Special personal thanks to Merrelyn Bates, for her generous and careful tuition of the authors in conflict managements and mediation; to Shirley Coyle, for her vision and her tireless work in developing the program within educational systems; and to Morag Morrison who was there at the beginning and is still pursuing the program's principles into new areas of children's need.

Particular thanks to the New South Wales Department of Education and Training — especially the Multicultural Programs Unit – and Education Queensland, and the staff and students of Alexandra Hills SHS, Bankstown PS, Bennett Road PS, Blackwell PS, Bremer SHS, Burwood GHS, Canterbury GHS, Canterbury PS, Casino HS, Casino West PS, Cleveland Street HS, Colyton HS, Crestmead SS, Erskine Park HS, Flagstone Community College, Homebush BHS, Homebush West PS, Kempsey South PS, MacGregor SHS, Marsden SHS, Marsden SS, Melville HS, Oxley Park PS, Rochedale SHS, Sandy Strait SS, Silkstone SS, Sir Joseph Banks HS, Summer Hill PS, Urangan SHS, Waterloo PS . . . and also to the new schools still joining and implementing the *Cooling Conflicts* and *Acting Against Bullying* programs. Thanks too to Hanya Stefaniuk, Amanda Burke and Greg Maguire of the Multicultural Programs Unit, and all the NSW Multicultural/ESL and Creative Arts Consultants, who have provided so much advice and assistance over the years. Thanks also to Education Queensland Policy Branch, particularly Carol Markie-Dadds and Chris Henderson.

Special thanks for the photographs to the teachers and students of Burwood GHS, Eltham College, Flagstone Community College, Rochedale SHS and St Peter's S Rochedale.

Thanks to Griffith University and the Australian Research Council, for their generous financial and resources support, and to Sharon Amos, Elio Gatti, Karen Green, Christine Hatton, Arthur Henry, Celia Moon, Maureen Owen, Kevin Smith, Jane Sizer and Jean Will, our trusty research teams.

Further thanks to all our drama, conflict management and mediation colleagues in the Swedish, Malaysian and Adelaide *DRACON* Projects, who provided us with many maps to help us understand the terrain: especially Mats Friberg, Anita Grunbaum, Margret Lepp, Horst Löfgren, Gitte Malm; Latif Kamaluddin and Janet Pillai; Dale Bagshaw, Rosemary Nursey-Bray and Ken Rigby.

Finally, thanks to all our colleagues and families, who have provided us with unswerving support in our endeavours over a very long time.

the program's principles

PART ONE

introduction

Cooling Conflict is a program to give students the tools to manage conflict and bullying. It uses a combination of drama and peer teaching, within the curriculum, in a whole-school context, to help the students themselves to change the culture of the school.

Central to this book is the principle that students can and should learn about conflict, its causes and effects in a morally neutral way, which takes out the blame and focuses on the behaviour. This approach allows a cognitive understanding of the structure of conflict, why conflicts happen, and possible ways of dealing with them. This principle generated the question that in turn has driven this whole project: if people – students – have this cognitive understanding, are they able to call on it to help them in real-life conflicts? The answer to this question was discovered through a combination of two strategies, drama and peer teaching, working together to create flexible, realistic, experimental models of human behaviour and new networks of personal and social understanding and support. Throughout the eight years of this action research, the answer has been a resounding 'yes'.

Whilst conflict generally may be inherent in human experience, it is not possible to be morally neutral about bullying. It's certainly a major form of conflict in social life, and a very high-profile one in schools. Some would say that, like conflict, bullying is part of human nature, but nobody would advocate tolerating it. The scholarship in the area, and all honest schools that know their students, acknowledge that bullying is an endemic problem, and none of the systems of bullying management in place are fully effective in dealing with it. However, by exploring conflict through drama, the *Cooling Conflict* program uncovered some new perspectives on bullying that suggested it might be possible to utilise drama's moral neutrality to help students unravel the tangle of confusing and unhelpful emotions aroused by bullying, and perhaps give them some useful cognitive understanding of the imbalance and misuse of power that lies at its heart, and the motives and processes that drive it. In this process it became evident that this cognitive understanding may even begin to change the social culture in a school.

A number of factors combine to make the approach explained in this book unique:

○ Conflict and bullying in schools are usually managed from the top down, whether by teachers, school administrations or students trained as prefects or peer mediators. *Cooling Conflict* puts the responsibility into the hands of the students themselves, thus empowering them, inviting and challenging them to change the very culture of schools.

○ Most conflict and bullying management in schools offers students moral precepts, retrospective sanctions and advice for the victims. This program offers the students cognitive understanding of conflict and bullying. They can utilise this understanding to prevent, de-escalate or resolve conflict and bullying.

○ Most anti-bullying programs in schools concentrate on the victim. This program acknowledges that conflict is a natural part of life, and bullying is a natural misuse of power, so it allows students to explore the issues in a value-free way that does not put them on the defensive either as bullies or victims. The program even avoids the word 'victim', wherever possible.

○ Most conflict and bullying management programs are extra-curricular, seen as part of the 'pastoral' responsibility of the school. This program sets the agenda right in the curriculum, using the relevant content of the curriculum itself – acknowledging that both conflict and the misuse of power inherent in bullying are actually in the core content of social knowledge, basic themes within many key learning areas in the classroom.

○ The program is designed to gradually change the culture of the whole-school community from the inside, developing networks of respect and support, with the students directly involved in the program as the leaders of the change from the top of the secondary school to the junior primary years.

○ The use of drama in conflict management is not new or original. There are drama handbooks for conflict resolution in psychotherapy contexts, and the use of drama techniques such as **role-play**, performance or simulation is often seen as valuable in many books and other resources on conflict handling and bullying. However, there is little serious research yet on its effectiveness – this program and this book are among the first attempts internationally to address this.

○ Where drama *is* used in conflict or bullying management, it is usually either as an ancillary tool or in ad hoc projects, driven by an enthusiastic teacher or a passing theatre team. This program centres its teaching on drama, and the development over the last 30 years of drama as a radical alternative pedagogy. More immediately, through the research the drama techniques have been refined into a well-tested, tightly-structured sequence that permits conflicts to be explored in depth, but one that is simple enough for non-specialist teachers and the students themselves to manage with comfort, using the hand-book provided in Part Two.

○ Similarly, peer teaching is recognised as a valuable learning tool in schools, but there is surprisingly little literature on it, and it has not been applied holistically to dealing with bullying or conflict, though it is beginning to be mentioned hopefully in some recent literature.

○ There are theoretical research texts on bullying and conflict in schools, and there are practical handbooks on how to deal with them. This book incorporates both, pinning a quite new and entirely accessible practice on an equally innovative theory that has been tested carefully through exhaustive and ongoing action research.

○ We believe that what gives this book its greatest value in the real school situation is the crucial link of drama with peer-teaching, and the development of this into a coherent system that can be applied not just in the isolated classroom, but within the curriculum, in a whole-school context.

The program's origins are a mixture of design and serendipity. The authors are drama teachers and educators, so for us to be interested in the relationship between drama and conflict is hardly surprising. The research for *Cooling Conflict* began by focusing on the relationship between conflict and drama in response to two approaches to us in the same year, one from the Peace and Development Research Institute in Gothenburg, Sweden, (known as the DRACON project) and the other from the New South Wales Whole-School Anti-Racism Project. Both were interested in investigating whether drama had anything to offer school students in the area of conflict resolution or management. Action research into this area seemed to be called for, allowing the researchers to get directly involved in classrooms. The *Cooling Conflict* project was not set up directly to solve a problem, but to implement a vision, using ourselves and other drama teachers as participant researchers, and documenting the research thoroughly to get useful critical feedback from all participants – students, teachers, observers, school administrators, parents – at key points. The project was conceived as a series of annual cycles of research, with each cycle being evaluated and the next re-planned in accordance.

The research started on a small scale, experimenting in one classroom with a willing drama class and an expert teacher, then spreading the following year to other classes in the same school through the introduction of peer teaching. After all, the students actually know much more about each other's conflicts than adults do – it is only two years since Year 11 students were in Year 9, and they remember the contexts and the pain of Year 9 conflicts, and also have usefully current advice for younger peers. Moreover, in many drama classrooms a lot of the action is through group-work and improvised, with the students sharing knowledge, planning and negotiating with each other. Some basic techniques of classroom drama are quite accessible and manageable by students themselves. Peer-teaching through drama has turned out for the vast majority of the students to be an enjoyable, enlightening and empowering experience, in some cases transformative – an experience in conflict management that is democratic and largely horizontal, not top-down. The students have a major say not only in their learning, but also in what they do with the knowledge and how they apply it in the school and other personal contexts. From the very first year, results showed that not only had the students grasped the basic concepts of conflict and what can be done about it to make it worse (escalate) or better (de-escalate), but that over 50 per cent of them were also attempting to utilise this knowledge in their own lives.

Another feature distinguished *Cooling Conflict* from most other conflict and bullying management strategies in schools: it happens within the curriculum, within the normal learning time. Most programs are extra-curricular, part of the pastoral structure of the school. Understandably, teachers prefer to think that conflict and bullying are behaviours that happen outside the classroom. *Cooling Conflict* uses the fact that both conflict and the misuse of power are highly relevant components of drama – of course – and also English, History, Human Relations Education, Citizenship Education, Aboriginal Studies, Legal Studies and even Science.

Since the second year of the project, the combination of drama and peer teaching within the normal curriculum have remained the core of *Cooling Conflict*. However, the implementation of the program has been continuously refined and expanded, spreading from just one class in one school to dozens of secondary and primary schools in New South Wales and Queensland involving thousands of students from Year 11 to Year 1.

The way it works is metaphorically like the concentric ripples spreading out from a stone dropped in water. Where the program is implemented to its maximum extent, it starts with senior secondary class, usually a drama class, learning through carefully structured drama techniques some basic concepts about conflict and bullying, and possible ways of managing them. These students teach the same concepts through the same techniques to some junior secondary students. In their turn, they teach classes of upper primary students. These upper primary classes have proved quite capable of grasping the concepts and the drama techniques well enough to teach Year 3 and 4 classes, who of course respond strongly to the drama and are themselves quite capable of taking in the basic and quite simple central concepts. There has been at least one successful attempt by Year 3s to teach even lower in the school, to Years 1 and 2.

The subject matter is mostly dictated by the students: in the peer teaching especially, the content is taken from those students who are the subjects of the learning, their own stories and contexts of conflict. Usually, the first – rather nervous – contact of the senior drama class with the younger students they will be teaching is not drama, but the rather safer activity of helping them to fill in a questionnaire. This often generates some preliminary discussion and storytelling, and therefore the beginning of a relationship, and a consequent relaxation of tension. In any case, it is always a pleasure to see the seniors poring over the questionnaires looking for starting points for the drama work, making connections with and sharing with their group their own so recent past. The conflicts are mostly within or near the students' own experience: conflicts at home between and among parents, children and siblings; in school between and among individual peers, groups or sets of students, teachers, boys versus girls; and within their neighbourhood: gangs, racial and ethnic tensions, bad neighbours, sports club rivalries and local class wars.

The recipients of the peer teaching at every level do learn something useful and have a good time doing so. However, the prime value of doing this is actually for the peer teachers themselves. Studies have shown that trying to teach something to somebody else is about the best possible way of fully grasping and remembering it. This is crystal clear in this program, borne out by all observations, and the frequent comments of the students themselves, and it is inspiring to see the reinforcement of learning and understanding that occurs as the students grapple with their responsibilities and gradually assume confidence and ownership of the intellectual capital. The peer teaching through drama has the advantage of sharing commonality of experience, together with the novelty of the event, underpinned by the safety net of greater seniority, age and esteem. The peer teachers usually start nervously, and grow in confidence and skill as they discover that the peer learners are not going to eat them alive. There is very rarely any disruptive behaviour, and it is not uncommon for strong relationships to be forged – in the first trial, one of the junior secondary classes became quite fixated on their peer teachers and most of them spent the next term hanging around the Year 11 room. The encounters between the secondary and primary schools are invariably a special occasion, whether the primary school receives a visit from their peer teacher neighbours, or they travel to the high school – which usually puts on a festive welcome as part of an induction day.

Throughout this program, the word **'conflict'** is used as the central defining term. Both the international DRACON research and the NSW Anti-Racism Program focused on the more specific theme of racial conflict, and our current research with Education Queensland is concentrated on bullying. However, to return to a point made earlier, in these potentially volatile and distressing subject areas, the term conflict is importantly value-neutral, and this has often provided a more viable starting point for exploration of racial conflict and bullying than to name and concentrate explicitly on those areas. In the stories and contexts suggested by the students, both racial issues and bullying come up inevitably, all the time, and each can be dealt with as just another manifestation of conflict. If 'racism' is the subject of the lesson, a set of moral values is implicated from the start, and students know what they are expected to do and say in the school environment, which may differ from their own position and that of their parents and community, so they come in with their defences prepared. It is the same with 'bullying'. Attitude change, or at least the opening up of attitudes to the possibility of dialogue and choice, is more likely if the students' attention is drawn to the action of conflict and bullying and exploring its consequences, so they can draw conclusions based on what they have vicariously experienced – racism or bullying becomes a factor in the dramatic story, not a 'position' to be attacked or defended. In this neutral context, we have been continually surprised how many participants have been willing to acknowledge having been at some time bullies as well as victims and bystanders.

Drama and peer teaching within a curriculum context have turned out to be two key sets of techniques that interact with each other to produce a pedagogy of classroom action and residual knowledge that is potent, and in some cases life-changing. In most cases there has been a demonstrable change of individual understanding and often there has been a change of ethos in the class and occasionally some personal transformation. It is too early to say yet whether this can transfer to the whole school or the community, but the story so far is worth the telling, which is what the first part of the book contains, along with the underpinning principles. In the second part of the book the structures and techniques for implementing *Cooling Conflict* are described in detail.

No heroes, no victims – just people

The principles underlying *Cooling Conflict*

CHAPTER 1

The *Cooling Conflict* program fundamentally depends on the students having a genuine cognitive understanding of the nature of conflict and bullying, and why and how they happen. Conflict is dealt with first, and many of the key concepts relating to conflict management apply equally to bullying. However, there are certain particular elements of bullying which are central to dealing with it effectively in schools, and these are examined separately.

The definitions and concepts explored in this chapter are derived from the extensive literatures on conflict resolution, mediation and bullying, but are simple enough for the students to grasp, remember and make use of.

Conflict management

If you cannot remove conflict from your life, why not adjust your thinking about it . . . why not try and see conflict as the salt of life . . . why not treat conflict as a form of life, particularly since we all know that it is precisely during the periods in our lives when we are exposed to a conflict that really challenges us, that we feel most alive.[1]

Throughout the program **conflict** is defined as: '. . . an opposition of ideas, interests, or actions that results in a struggle over status, power and/or resources'.[2]

There is nothing intrinsically bad about conflict. Conflict acknowledges or makes explicit the tensions between competing forces, and 'the absence of conflict may signal apathy, disinterest, non-involvement and alienation'.[3] Conflict offers the opportunity for humans to respond to its challenges, to seek new pathways and change perspectives. The emotion people invest in dealing with conflict may provide the energy and impetus that help to resolve it, sidestep it, reconfigure it so it is no longer a conflict – or just live with it. Conflict can give us valuable new insights into our lives, and the lives and values of those around us. Moreover, not all conflicts can be fully resolved; some sets of clashing interests or power relationships are beyond the protagonists' powers to alter; some antagonists cannot be finally appeased. These are reasons why this program avoids the commonly used phrase 'conflict resolution' in favour of the more even-handed words 'management' or 'handling'.

The problem with conflict, what causes distress, is that it easily becomes egotistical, when our emotions, interests and values become invested in an issue so wholly that we cannot recognise or accept that other people's may be different. Often the power relationship is unbalanced so as to obscure the substantive issues at stake and heat the emotions further. The frustration of conflict badly handled can then severely damage the participants.

A basic tenet used in the program to help the students grasp the nature and diversity of conflict and its undesirable manifestations is that they can occur in any context of human life, at any level of society. Conflicts happen:

- within one person, internally – e.g. where competing desires and interests cause distress and confusion
- between individuals, in interpersonal relationships – e.g. couples, colleagues, family
- between groups – e.g. timber workers and environmental protesters
- between communities – e.g. different cultural groups in a city
- within the international arena – e.g. over territorial fishing rights, and geo-political matters, from terrorism to inter-boundary warfare
- in more abstract and generic ways, culturally based in the broadest sense – e.g. based on race, gender, socio-economic factors.

The main basic elements of any dispute are clashes of **interests**, **rights** and **power**,[4] or some form of **misunderstanding**. **Interests** are the things that people want, demand or claim. They include the underlying motivations and can be substantive (either tangible – e.g. money – or intangible – e.g. equality), psychological, (e.g. feelings of acceptance, loss of face), or procedural (e.g. fairness in the process). **Rights** are the standards or values that define what is fair and appropriate or determines what parties are entitled to. They may be determined by legislation (e.g. laws and codes of conduct), established by societal norms (e.g. shelter and food), or set by personal values. **Power** is associated with authority, status, influence or control of finance and resources. Identifying the power issues is essential, as is being aware of our own power within the conflict management process itself. If this is not accounted for then escalation can occur and may lead to aggression, threats, retaliation and violence. Because of the fear frequently associated with power, the issues may stay unresolved and fester. One of the most important questions to establish in any conflict is 'Who is powerless?' It is worth noting that conflict is also sometimes caused by a clash between these elements – as when a person's **interests** are threatened by their lack of **power**.

The fourth cause of conflict, **misunderstanding**, should in theory be the easiest to resolve. In practice misunderstandings are frequently quite hard to disentangle, for two reasons at least. They inevitably invoke the perception that a right, interest or power position is at stake, and this causes behaviour that often escalates the conflict with the other party. Moreover, a misunderstanding is much more likely to occur if the cultural pre-conditions are present. With people we know, understand and empathise with, we have a stake in ensuring we do understand their rights, interests and power, and our positive relationship depends on sustaining good understanding. Those whom we are programmed by our stereotyped attitudes to mark out as 'other' and 'alien', we are likely to misunderstand, as we misread their actions according to our constructs rather than their own motives. Further misunderstandings then become part of the very fabric of the conflict itself.

Once a conflict is under way, further developments have the potential to occur. It does not take much for conflict to **escalate**. People can become emotional and react quickly. Sometimes they get stuck in their positions and reach a point where the original issue is lost in other issues. It is difficult to remain rational and unemotional in conflict. All the parties have their own perceptions and their own sense of personal investment in the issue. Each then makes assumptions about the other party's motives, values and behaviours. These can easily become subsumed into emotional fears (particularly of losing power). Tolerance is extinguished and once this has occurred the conflict has escalated. As the interaction becomes more complex and difficult to comprehend the individuals involved in the conflict tend to simplify it by finding only one problem and one main source – the other party.[5] The **antagonist** becomes depersonalised and eventually demonised, which makes communication even less likely.

Conflicts tend to **escalate** in quite clearly identifiable phases, which have been variously described. As we have indicated, we found a simple, three-phase description of escalation very manageable by the students, and appropriate to their needs. **Latent conflict** is the first stage, where the conditions for conflict exist – a potential tension of interests, rights or power, which has not yet reached the stage of a clash. This is characterised by most or all of those affected being quite unaware of any problem. **Emerging conflict**, the next stage, is where those conditions are forming themselves into a clash. In this stage, some of those affected are dimly or partially aware of the conflict. Often, it is those on the edge, or outside the conflict, who can see it most clearly, rather than the protagonists who are bound up in their egocentric positions. **Manifest conflict** is the stage when the conflict is resulting in action that is visible and unmistakable to all, usually with anger and frustration and often violence.

In any conflict, it takes two to escalate the conflict. Action is always followed by response. Responses too, can be categorised:

○ **Avoidance** – withdrawing from the conflict, pretending it is not happening
○ **Accommodation** – giving in and yielding to the pressure
○ **Assertion** – facing the problem, highlighting the discrepancies and maintaining one's position
○ **Aggression** – returning force and antipathy in equal measure, or more.

The likelihood of any one of these responses is partly determined by the individual, partly by their cultural programming. Especially in the early stages of a manifest conflict, any response is likely to lead to escalation. However, some responses are more likely than others to be able eventually or in the longer term to contribute to defusing or resolving the conflict – **de-escalating** it, as it is called.

Perceptions and assumptions about motives and values play an important part in the development of conflict. Differences in interests – whether substantive, psychological or procedural – may be real or perceived, and so may the antagonist's opinions or purposes. It is often impossible for protagonists embroiled in bitter conflict to verify whether their perceptions of their antagonist's attitudes and behaviour are accurate, or the product of their own assumptions or generalised stereotypes of 'the other'. Dismantling misperceptions, and particularly de-demonising the antagonist, is sometimes the task of others, third parties outside or on the edge of the conflict, who have the combination of distance and empathy that enables them to understand the behaviour and respect the needs of both parties. This process is called **mediation**.

It is often inadvisable, if other times and places are available, to intervene directly in a person-to-person conflict, when tempers are running hot – unless the combatants are likely to damage each other and the mediator knows that s/he can prevent that without getting hurt in the process. The first step is to help the protagonists break out of their ego-centrism, which usually entails talking to the parties separately, and then perhaps acting as go-between, starting the process of dismantling assumptions and negotiating trade-offs. Only then may it be possible to restore direct communication and move to a point of mediating through the conflict. For these reasons the *Cooling Conflict* program has embedded within the central drama technique an 'extension scene' which allows and encourages mediation to occur.

The extent and depth to which all these principles of conflict and mediation are investigated and taught in the program varies enormously according to the length of time and the maturity of the participants. The whole must be broken down to what might be manageable at each level, and what common fundamentals could underpin everybody's knowledge. In cognitive terms, this boils down to a skeletal model consisting of simple statements of names, categories and definitions in the form of a checklist.

The conflict concepts

☐ **Conflict** derives from clashes of **interests**, **rights** and **power**.

☐ Conflicts are often fuelled by **misunderstanding** based on assumptions and **stereotyping**. Cultural conflicts are often fuelled by stereotypes based on recognition of difference without recognition of commonality, combined with fear or ignorance of the perceived difference.

☐ Conflicts have three identifiable **escalating** stages:

1. **Latent** or 'hidden' conflict, when there are present underlying conditions of potentially conflicting interests and rights, or attitudes of misunderstanding, but these have not yet led to conscious clashes because the conflict is still hidden from its protagonists

2. **Emerging** or '**brewing**' conflict, where some but not all of those affected by conflict are aware of it

3. **Manifest**, or 'open' conflict, where the clashes of interests, rights or power are there for all those affected, and outsiders, to see.

☐ Conflicts naturally tend to **escalate** because of the emotions involved, and **de-escalation** has to take account of the emotional conditions as well as the clashes and misunderstandings.

☐ Some conflicts need third party intervention, or **mediation**.

☐ Mediation is often best undertaken by separating the parties and finding what can be conceded or negotiated away from a moment of confrontation.

☐ Not all conflicts are destructive – conflict can be healthy.

☐ The central participants in the clashes of interests, rights and power are known as the **protagonists**. To each protagonist, the person or persons with whom they are in conflict are their **antagonists**.

It is left to the drama itself to expound and clarify this model and these concepts in the minds of the students, up to whatever level they are capable of, in whatever time is available. That is one of the powers of drama, as may be seen in Chapter 2 – it brings the model to life, makes the skeleton dance.

Difference, culture and conflict

A word pivotal to the program is 'difference'. On the one hand, it fuels conflict and particularly bullying. To be different is to risk and suffer misunderstanding, one of the principal roots of conflict. To be different in schools is also often enough to incur bullying, as children jostle for identity and acceptance in the dominant group culture. This is plainly often a major motivation for the complicit bystander, frequently too scared to risk being labelled 'different' by aiding the bullied. Instead, bystanders often seek approval by encouraging the teasing, thereby enjoying the security of the pack. Difference, and particularly cultural difference, is a key concept that must be explored in any analysis of both conflict and bullying. This is one further reason why drama is the key method used – it allows notions of kinship and difference, empathy and alienation, to be explored both cognitively and emotionally in a penalty-free context, realistic but divorced from the consequences of real-life difference.

Children learn how to label and categorise others as being 'similar' or 'different' from themselves at three and four years of age, from such sources as the media and their parents. By this age they are aware of gender differences, as well as which group they belong to. In learning the various labels that are attached to people from differing backgrounds, they also learn the evaluations that go along with them. The perspectives of the majority culture become dominant and influential. While young children's key relationship is with their parents, by the age of 11 and 12 they are adopting the ethnic perspectives and attitudes that are held by the adult community. Furthermore, children take on board negative attitudes about groups that are targets of prejudice. Thus, the way children perceive social groups is largely based on their cognitive and moral development, which in turn is influenced by parents, peers and media outlets.

Educators need to be aware of the possible dangers that can arise when placing people into categories. It may be better to focus on similarities in children's experiences rather than highlighting differences, especially in the early grades of school, placing emphasis on developing a feeling of 'we' within which there is great diversity. In higher grades, students will be more cognitively able to understand that being different is not intrinsically bad, and that differences between people exist on a variety of levels – when older they can hold a multitude of perspectives. The ability grows to place themselves in another person's position, where the 'other' is seen in relationship to 'self' – and with the expectation that the other person can do the same. In some children this understanding develops in the final years of primary school, though others may not develop it until adolescence well and truly sets in. At that age peer group acceptance becomes a central concern. One must be liked in order to feel confident and for positive self-esteem to be fostered.

The term 'conflict' itself has no simple definition; its meanings are varied across cultural groups. In addition, the strategies accessed to bring about resolution are also often dissimilar. However, we have the potential to learn and gain a great deal of understanding about conflict management from other cultures. In allowing other cultures to educate and inform us, we can equip ourselves with numerous strategies as well as a multitude of new perspectives in which to view and manage not only our own conflicts, but also those of the people around us. Furthermore, it is ignorant to presume that one culture alone possesses the correct way of dealing with disputes. If we disregard the wisdom of others, we are in fact doing ourselves an injustice by limiting our own knowledge and wisdom.

Enhancement, not elimination, of human diversity must be our goal. Diversity can be a source of harmony, rather than a source of conflict. Uniformity can destroy rather than advance civilisation. A single world culture is not a desirable goal. Continuity and congruence with their cultural history connect persons and groups to their own particular depths, their own unique wisdom, and their own particular configuration of human archetypes, religious symbols and central values.[6]

Bullying

As with conflict, there is a generally agreed definition of **bullying** which is used in the literature worldwide.

Bullying is repeated oppression, psychological or physical, of a less powerful person by a more powerful person or group of persons.[7]

The eight years of research that inform *Cooling Conflict* have produced a myriad of students' own stories of conflict, many of which have involved bullying and power abuse. These stories have led to the innovative principles which address bullying in the program – in conjunction with extensive reading, discussion with teachers, experts on bullying and education officials, plus the impressive range of available resources, books, websites, films and CDs.

While many anti-bullying strategies work to some extent, none are wholly effective, and some even seem to increase bullying. What makes addressing bullying even more difficult – but is not so clearly or universally acknowledged – is that the links between the incidence of bullying and the reporting of it are at best tenuous. All we do know is that the incidence of serious bullying reported by students in schools throughout the developed world over the past decade has remained remarkably consistent at 10%.

The word bullying is so strongly emotive, negatively so, that people's reaction to the word itself drives their responses, particularly in public, or when they are under scrutiny. Some schools are very defensive and prefer not to acknowledge that there is any bullying going on – understandably concerned for their reputation among the parents and community. Others have put in place high-profile anti-bullying plans that only work to the extent to which they can make their reality and their actual commitment match their rhetoric.

Most anti-bullying strategies concentrate on the victim of bullying, trying to give help to the afflicted. A few acknowledge that the causes of bullying lie in the unequal and unjust misuse of power, but tend to focus this knowledge again on helping the victim. There is very much less attention given to addressing the causes of conflict, and almost none to helping the bully. *Cooling Conflict* avoids this focus on the victim and on blame and uses drama techniques to address bullying as it addresses conflict generally, in a value-neutral way. A basic principle is that all human action has its rationale and its integrity, and some aspect of this can be explored and revealed through drama. This is often approached indirectly – as it must be in those situations where angels fear to tread. The program removes the blame and considers all those misuses of power labelled as bullying to be human events where, depending on context, all of us could be implicated as one of the three parties (a **bully**, a **bystander** or a victim, who is referred to in this program as a **bullied**, for reasons that will be explained). The students are challenged to answer two questions: could the bully in one situation be a victim in another, and a bystander in a third? Are there particular characteristics that pre-dispose certain people to being victimised or to bullying?

The list of concepts about bullying which is taught in *Cooling Conflicts* is longer than the generic conflict one, but this cognitive armoury is proving just as valuable to the students and just as easily grasped and memorised.

Central to the dramatic explorations are some of the same concepts – and the same useful jargon – as we explored in our generalised conflict project. Difference and the **stereotyping** of the different, of course, are a key cause. **Bullying** too can usefully be identified in three stages of **latent**, **emerging** and **manifest**. Bullying can be **escalated** and needs to be **de-escalated**. Some bullying needs **mediation**, and third-party intervention. Students are often quite willing to acknowledge themselves as bullies in particular contexts (because they are absolved from being thereby cast as odious in themselves); a significant number of students disclose privately to their teachers or peer teachers, in the protective shade of the drama, that they have been victims of bullying, or complicit bystanders.

The bullying concepts

- **Bullying** is always a bad thing, but it is a form of human behaviour that exists in all societies and social contexts.

- Bullying can be defined as the *ongoing misuse of an imbalance of power causing disempowerment, fear, suffering or humiliation to other(s) less powerful*.

- Bullying and harassment can be *physical* (being hit, tripped, pinched), *verbal* (name-calling, teasing, putdowns), *psychological* (gestures, threats, being stalked), *social* (ostracisation or having rumours spread) or *sexual* (physical, verbal or nonverbal sexual conduct).

- People bullying always perceive their actions to be in their own **interest**, but are always infringing the **rights** of the **bullied**.

- Bullying is always egotistic and never empathic; it usually emphasises difference of the person being bullied from the dominant power group, and stereotypes that person.

- There are three parties to bullying ('the three Bs'):

  - the **bully** (or bullies), who misuses power

  - the **bullied** who suffer the misuse of power

  - the complicit **bystander** (or bystanders), who permits or approves the bullying.

  (Note that the bystander may be one or more human beings, or may be an institution or agency that encourages or tolerates bullying, or allows it to continue.)

- All humans have the capacity to be **bully**, **bullied**, or **bystander** depending on the context. Some contexts and personal characteristics may be predisposed to arouse particular actions or responses.

- Many bullies and bystanders are unaware of their roles, or of the distress to the bullied.

- Situations of bullying, because they are ongoing, **escalate** over time, and can be seen to have three identifiable stages:

    – **latent** (where the imbalance of power exists, but the parties are not aware of misuse)

    – **emerging** (where some but not all of the protagonists recognise bullying is taking place)

    – **manifest** (where suffering is caused to the bullied with the knowledge of the persons bullying and the bystanders).

- Each bully, bullied and bystander bears some **responsibility** and has some **power** to **de-escalate** or end the bullying.

- Strategies for all three parties to address bullying include:

    – **confronting** and acknowledging the bullying

    – **avoiding** the bullying situation

    – **mediating** or appealing to others to assist in ending the bullying.

- Some bullying situations can be addressed by the parties involved, if there is willingness among all three parties to address the questions of interest, rights and power; others, where there is no willingness, need **mediation** (third-party) intervention.

The word 'victim' has been replaced by 'bullied', because 'victim' is so imbued with emotive overtones. Speaking of the bullied allows the students to accept the concept in a relatively cooler terms, so that they might even be able to step back from the notion of victimhood and examine the whole question of the victim being – usually, but by no means always, very unwillingly – an active party in the bullying (and therefore capable of action).

No heroes, no victims – conflict management in the program

The students are invariably very interested in this conceptual framework, and the most important outcome of the drama work is the follow-up reflective discussion. This often starts during the drama itself – where the structure actually makes room for it within the dramatic context. Students regularly embark on cogent, sustained discussion clarifying, contesting, questioning and pulling apart the theory, in terms of their own experience and the imminent necessity of processing it in order to teach it to others. Some of the best and most reinforcing discussion happens post hoc, when the **peer teachers** compare notes on how they have dealt with the conflicts, and the questions, of their learners.

Detailed exposition of just what the students learn about conflict and what uses they put that to, is in Chapter 3. As will appear there, the thing that just about everybody learns is the names of the three stages, however superficially. The students enjoy learning and using the jargon, which gives them a starting point to shape and label what for them is a common, distressing and confusing part of their lives. Although the program also gives alternative, more common labels to the stages – 'hidden' for latent, 'brewing' for emerging – the schools invariably use the more 'technical' terms, because they have more importance and status, and the students revel in parading their new-found expertise:

Miss, Miss! There's a manifest conflict on the bus!

Often the teachers, too, enjoy sharing their new joint knowledge:

[to the class, rebuking a student's misbehaviour] *I think there might be a conflict emerging between Lawrence and me . . .*

One crucial conceptual problem that will arise is the tendency for students, particularly younger ones, initially to see and portray the conflict as a simple battle between good and evil, particularly if bullying is involved. The protagonist is invariably the innocent victim and potential hero, the bully invariably bad, mean and enjoying it. Some drama strategies can tend to reinforce this simplistic division of goodies and baddies. However, manipulating the use of role and point of view within drama can result in the participants being given the opportunity to see all points of view. Accordingly there are some 'hero exterminating' techniques built into the central dramatic strategy. There are no heroes, only people, who can respond well or badly in a context according to their character. During the dramatic scenes, the 'villain' often has to explain if not justify the behaviour, and obviously 'I hurt people because I like it' will not satisfy. This does need sensitive teaching, to encourage the audience to probe: 'Enjoying hurting people is not natural – what started you off?' Once they are alerted to the problem, the peer teachers usually realise that in the initial devising stages the dramatic villain must be better **backgrounded**. The program reminds students that 'you must find that person's integrity, find out what made them that way'. In the peer teaching, they can then themselves apply pressure against any glib and black-and-white responses.

Drama has proved a valuable and straightforward way of experiencing, crystallising and making the concepts explicit. However, the basic drama strategies need to be used organically, rather than in isolation, as is often the case with drama used in conflict resolution. The drama needs to help the students see beyond the immediate surface of conflicts, especially young students: though they are quick to pick up the idea of the three stages, their notions of conflict's roots and significance must be extended. Here is a typical first draft situation devised by young students:

Scene 1 – Two groups of students of different ethnic origin in the yard at the beginning of recess look suspiciously at each other and mutter threats (latent).

Scene 2 – A student from one group walks past the other and is tripped up, which starts a scuffle between the victim and the tripper (emerging).

Scene 3 – This draws the attention of all the members of both groups, who close in on each other in a free-for-all (manifest).

It shows some understanding certainly – there is a basic grasp of the escalation of conflict through the three stages. However, in reality it is all just the onset of a manifest conflict. The students need to be encouraged to see the roots of conflict as being much deeper and less spontaneous. This may be as simple as imposing a time constraint: there has to be at least one week time lapse between each scene. Such a constraint automatically encourages the students to flesh out the conflict and find more substantial motivations and causes for the conflict. Of the three stages, understanding the 'latent' stage is by far the hardest for the students. It is the most abstract, of course. The other two stages can be directly characterised by actions and words, while latent conflict can only be made explicit as sub-text of something else. Its relative complexity can be seen even in the conflict checklist above, where the definition of 'latent' is far longer and lumpier than the other two.

In the latest stage of the research project, where for the first time we have been working with primary students at length and in detail, some of the teachers have identified an interesting phenomenon that is probably related to the students' level of maturation, and also the nature of their conflicts, which tend to be spontaneous, reacting to the moment rather than deeply held perspectives of interests, rights and power. Students below Year 5, and even some Year 5s, have difficulty in grasping the concept of latent conflict or bullying, but with the right help, they can. One unexpectedly sophisticated scenario came from a Year 5 group, whose scene of 'manifest' conflict initially puzzled the watching teacher: two men who had broken into a house were stealing a baby. 'Is this even conflict?' wondered the teacher. The 'emerging' scene was equally ambiguous – the men breaking into the house. Only when the 'latent' scene was revealed did the penny drop – the men were being fired from work the week before, by the house-owner and baby's father.

Another very impressive metaphor for conflict emerged during a primary teaching session, though whether from the primary students or their secondary peer teachers we are not able to say. Conflict was compared with a volcano, where the dormant volcano represented latent conflict, the smoke and rumblings of a volcano about to erupt represented emerging conflict, and the eruption represented manifest. Certainly there was a clear understanding of latency and the three stages demonstrated in this elegant analogy.

One feature of the teaching – again partly due to maturation and language levels, and partly presumably also to the 'trickle-down' effect of the concepts becoming more shorthand as they are transmitted – is that the adjective becomes a noun in itself.

As you can see, we've got some latent here, and it could become an emerging.

Mostly this kind of shorthand is innocuous, but sometimes, with the younger children, it diverts the participants entirely away from the purpose of the learning, as with the group that never used the word 'conflict' and devised three scenes of a comet striking earth, where the comet strike was 'the manifest', the comet heading for earth 'the emerging' and the comet sailing through space 'the latent'. While this shows some considerable structural and semantic understanding, there's no context of conflict at all.

One unfortunate, quite rare but quite inevitable phenomenon of the program is meta-conflict – real conflict among the participants, usually arising during the rehearsal period, but occasionally during the peer teaching sessions. There is considerable tension combined with very challenging tasks in both these settings, and naturally the tension spills over occasionally into emerging or even manifest conflict, and at least temporary bullying among the conflict managers! Quite often the very realisation may be enough to defuse the immediate tension in shared amusement. Normally, working groups for the peer teaching should be chosen by friendship, to avoid possible friction.

Given the amount of tension in the peer teaching, together with the complexity and challenge of the tasks, the amount of real conflict is very slight. The urgency and the grown-up importance of the peer teaching task help to keep groups unified. So too the use of drama techniques, through that dramatic oscillation between distance and empathy: much of the action of the classroom consists of distancing oneself from real life in order to pretend to take on realistic roles, that themselves demand real emotion and empathy. As in any other real conflict, separation and time for reflection can prove the answer, as in the following humble, perceptive and magnanimous student journal entry:

I am really disappointed though in myself and in Sophie for the way we both acted in front of the class – the whole idea of the day was to manage conflict. So I would like to apologise to you Miss Mac for behaving that way. I would also like to apologise to the other people in my group.

Notes

1. Augsburger, D. (1992) *Conflict Mediation Across Cultures: Pathways and Patterns*. Louisville, KY: Westminster, p. 4.

2. Opotow, S. (1991) Adolescent Peer Conflicts. Implications for Students and for Schools. *Education and Urban Society*, vol. 23, no. 4, p. 416.

3. Johnson, D. & Johnson, F. (1991) *Joining Together. Group Theory and Group Skills* (4th edn). Englewood Cliffs, NJ: Prentice Hall.

4. Alternative Dispute Resolution Branch (1999) *Conciliation Skills Training*. Brisbane: Dept of Justice & Attorney-General.

5. Kellgren, H. (1996) *A Model for Conflict Escalation*. Penang: DRACON Seminar: unpublished paper.

6. Augsburger, D. op. cit., p. 206.

7. Rigby, K. (1996) *Bullying in Schools – and what to do about it*. Melbourne: ACER, p. 15.

The program's
strategies
Drama and peer teaching

CHAPTER 2

Drama

Drama and conflict

Drama is the art form that most explicitly mirrors and explicates human conflict. Conflict is part of the basic business of drama, which exists to depict and explore human relationships. Key words and concepts are shared between drama and conflict resolution. The very words **protagonist** and **antagonist** that are used to label the main parties in a conflict derive from Greek drama. A central element of drama is *tension*, and the impetus towards the final *resolution* of that tension. Dramatic action consists of *dialogue, opposition, negotiation, argumentation*; all employed in the drive towards resolution of tension in theatre and in conflict.

Humans are storying beings who select, order and attempt to control their social and personal reality in terms of on-going narratives. Drama works by constructing a fictional narrative of particular on-going relationships and conflicts, which may be controlled and changed at the will of the playwrights or participants. These fictional narratives are constructed in the very way in which real conflicts are construed. The three conflict definitions – **latent**, **emerging** and **manifest** – that are used by conflict mediators, and that we use in the program to describe the phases of escalation, also describe the shape of classic drama: from seeds of conflict, to action and escalation in which the conflict emerges and is made manifest, and in the steps taken by the characters to de-escalate and resolve the conflict – successfully in comedy, unsuccessfully (without the help of the gods) in tragedy!

Furthermore, all the areas of situation and relationship that are explored through dramatic action are central to real-life understanding and stable relationships. Drama is about the clashes and conflicts of *personality*, of *values*, of *attitudes*, of *emotions*, of *interests* both internal and environmental, of *philosophy* and *ideology*, of *ethics* and *morals*.

Drama in fact provides models of human behaviour and human relationships. Like the models of the globe or the human skeleton in geography and anatomy, drama depicts in simplified form the contours of human relationships and conflict, so that the important structural features can be seen. The components of the conflict can be taken apart, the causes and consequences analysed and experimented with, the model reassembled and changed. Even more effectively than the globe and skeleton, drama animates the model. Drama incorporates not just the physical shape of the conflict, but the emotional content and subjective meanings for the characters involved.

Drama and education: the background

From earliest times, drama and theatre have had a long relationship with education and teaching. By 'earliest times' we mean both historical (in traditional societies, performances that conveyed and reinforced a community's lore, history and social mores) and developmental (dramatic play is one of the first and most potent ways children learn). In recent decades, many manifestations of drama have been used in community and schools settings not just to convey messages colourfully, but as tools of learning engagement. Two of these movements, 'drama in education' and 'theatre for development', are of particular importance to this program, as they provide the dramatic forms that we have shaped into the instruments for the students to learn how to cool conflict. They share two crucial characteristics: a strong agenda for social consciousness-raising and change, and the desire to break down the 'fourth wall' of western theatre and engage the audience as participants. Both, incidentally, have been around since the early 1970s.

Theatre for development has emerged in developing countries, as a way of focusing educationally and economically disadvantaged communities on ways of improving their lives, health and conditions. It is seen as a natural way to communicate with people who may have little access to literate media, radio or television. It may be used for officially sanctioned purposes (for raising consciousness about sanitation or the environment, dispelling myths about HIV-AIDS, and teaching villagers more used to hieratic or chiefly rule the basic principles of democratic voting) or for unofficial ones (protest and combating economic or political oppression).

In early forms, theatre for development tended to be very didactic in approach and style – groups of outsiders travelling round communities usually performing a play with a message in a western style of theatre. More recently, this has been seen to be patronising and often counter-productive, generating resistance to the outsiders and their alien message that runs counter to traditional community practice. Accordingly, a more participatory approach has emerged, involving theatrical facilitators coming into a community for an extended period, to listen to the community's concerns and needs, and explore with them the possibilities and threats inherent in their health, environmental or political contexts. More participatory techniques of theatre are being used, and often the facilitators will incorporate the community's own traditional performance forms of dance and song, storytelling and praise poetry.

One of the most influential forms of theatre for development, **theatre of the oppressed**, was formulated and popularised by the Brazilian liberation theatre director **Augusto Boal**.[1] He has always sought a participatory role for his audiences, not least in consulting them to generate the stories that form the basis of the plays. His most celebrated technique, **forum theatre**, still consists of a play devised by actors to an audience, but it involves that audience, whom he re-named '**spect-actors**', in active intervention and discussion. *Cooling Conflicts* uses *forum theatre* as its basic drama technique.

Drama in education is usually seen in school classrooms and often in English, History or Human Relations Education lessons. It has a long history, and is often associated with the British pioneer drama educators **Dorothy Heathcote** and **Gavin Bolton**.[2] It is based on the improvised dramatic forms of children's play and structured role-play. The participants are all characterised as collaborative learners, and together with their teacher they set up and explore fictional dramatic situations 'as if . . .' they were happening. They make the drama from the inside as the characters in those situations – working simultaneously as actors, playwrights and directors. They use a mix of **experiential role-play** (where the players are absorbed in the situation, empathising with their roles) and more **distanced** theatrical rehearsal techniques, to find out the dynamics of the situation, and its causes and consequences. There is no external audience; the teacher is often engaged in the drama as a character, helping to shape the learning from the inside. Scenes may involve all the class; sometimes a scene may be enacted simultaneously by several groups, or by the students in pairs. This kind of drama is now often collectively known as '**process drama**' as it concentrates entirely on the process, and there is no product, in the form of a play to be watched by others. We have used *process drama* techniques as the enhancements to the basic forum theatre.

Drama and role theory

Though the function of drama is to simplify moments of life so that they can be comprehended on a stage or acting space, drama is actually more complex than real life in one way, in the way it engages three quite distinct contexts simultaneously: the *real life context*, the fictional *dramatic context* and the *context of the performance*. The participants have three sets of roles. Their interaction and overlay of these on each other, the invocation and suspension of each of them, are what provide the learning potential:

1. The participants in *real life* are, say, 30 thirteen year olds living in New South Wales. On a day-by-day basis their roles as children, family members and students are fixed.

2. In the *fictional dramatic context* they take the roles of characters, the roles that determine the nature and the narrative of the play. In this context their real life roles are at least partially suspended, to allow the dramatic narrative to unfold – they may be bullies, or those who need help, or who otherwise are in conflict, and of course there are no consequences in the real context, because the conflicts and the roles are fictional.

3. In the *context of performance*, which here is the drama lesson, they have another set of roles: as playwrights, directors, actors and audience of the play they are engaged in creating together. Here they experiment in earnest with the very notion of role. This includes:

   –techniques of renegotiating aspects of the dramatic situation, of role-reversal, of experimenting with different actions to improve or change the role and introducing new characters. These are all part of the *playwright*'s devices.

   –reshaping the audience point of view to provide more distance or more empathy, changing the physical parameters, accentuating the dramatic irony, or providing new internal insights as part of the *director*'s repertoire.

   –adopting a variety of postures, changing the energy level and responding in a range of ways, sometimes surprisingly, which are all part of the *actor*'s box of tricks.

   –watching the action from inside or outside, deliberately changing one's point of view on the situation, sitting down in post-drama de-briefing, discussion and reflection, and even re-creating the experience in another art form – painting, poetry and song, or writing. These reflective responses are all part of the *audience*'s repertoire.

Player and audience

Drama centrally depends on an emotion equally central to conflict resolution, namely **empathy**: the ability to identify not only cognitively but affectively with others – to step into others' shoes to some degree, and temporarily see the world from an alien viewpoint. Drama actually works through the simultaneous operation of **empathy** and **distance**. The 'dual affect',[3] whereby the participant 'weeps in play as a patient, but revels as the player' permits simultaneous emotional identification and closeness to the conflict and dispassionate awareness of the elements of that conflict, as many writers on drama have pointed out.

Drama also permits the point-of-view and its accompanying emotional orientation to be changed or switched. This can take place within the conflict itself from **protagonist** to **antagonist**. The point of view and emotional engagement can also move in a drama from the central event of the conflict to the edge, becoming fixed on the supporting characters, interested onlookers or chorus. The focus may also switch to outside the conflict and finally to the onlookers or audience. Participants may be asked to act out a situation to an audience of other participants – a scene they have prepared, or one that they have already role-played experientially. The actors remain in their roles while the audience then become active participants and interview the characters, finding out more about them or giving them advice. Only one step further, and the audience may be invited to intervene in the action itself – and this turns the role-play effectually into **forum theatre** and the audience into '**spect-actors**'.

Following from the above, a drama can incorporate both audience and actor within its essential structure – embodying the roles and points-of-view of the participant and the observer.

Sub-text and metaphor in drama

Drama works through exploring and making manifest *sub-text*. In real life the sub-texts of interactions and relationships are always implicit (that's what *sub*-text means). These sub-texts include the relative status of the participants, their motivations, attitudes, emotional orientations to each other, and the latent and incipient conflicts which those engender. In drama, the sub-texts drive and control the action, and the condensation of time, place and action enables the cause and effect of these sub-texts to be made explicit, or to resonate with the real lives of the participants. In other words, we can perceive those things that for various reasons lie unspoken or cannot be said.

Particularly in conflict scenarios, the text and the sub-text may directly contradict each other as sets of motives conflict, and the characters become more self-centred and less honest with each other or themselves. Drama permits these contradictions to be made visible. More than that, through the operation of dramatic irony, the contradiction can be highlighted for cool examination, and for the interpolation of humour and distance to illuminate the emotional landscape.

Drama is always at least one remove from real life. Some forms can remain quite close to real experience, and quite personal and direct, while others generalise the experience into indirect, more metaphorical and universally recognised experience (at least within the shared culture or cultures of the participants). Similarly, there are contrasts and connections between the various forms of classroom drama and the theatre in terms of the interaction: between on the one hand exploring and experiencing a dramatic situation and on the other fixing it in a reproducible form for communication or performance on stage or film.

The dramatic contract

Before any dramatic event can happen, the participants must agree to abide by the basic *contract* of drama, which is that they will share the willing suspension of their disbelief in order to enter together the fictional world of the drama. Put simply, if all the participants do not accept the fiction, then the fictional world cannot be created – drama can only happen voluntarily, at the will of all the participants. This is important for another reason, that drama provides a 'safe space', where the participants agree that whatever happens in the fictional and real-life contexts will remain distinct. The fictional conflicts that the characters have will not be translated back into the participants' real lives (and conversely, the tensions and affections of real life will be suspended in the interest of keeping the fiction authentic). Drama is above all an ensemble art form, depending on all participants playing their part to create a unified whole.

Therefore, preconditions have to be established. The first of these is to create the *context of performance*. In traditional theatre, this is ready-made: a specially designed building called a theatre, where at particular times people come together specifically and purposefully to perform and watch plays. A classroom is not like that: it was designed for other purposes entirely, for other methods of teaching and learning; in these terms, drama is rarely part of the normal purposes of its inhabitants. Physically, at the very least, some reorganisation of the furniture is likely to be needed; in terms of purpose, the inhabitants all need to recognise and accept that the purpose of teaching and learning will be now best carried out by drama.

Next, participants have to be helped to establish and accept the contract. An ensemble must be created. There must be trust that the other participants will honour the rules of the performance context, and work to make the fictional context authentic. Sometimes these rules need to be spelt out and agreed explicitly. Often, dramatic games and exercises are used, firstly as 'ice-breakers', then more specifically to develop trust and concentration, or to focus on the particular theme of the drama work to be undertaken.

It is crucial that students are enabled to focus intellectually and emotionally so that they can operate and respond appropriately, particularly if they are asked to adopt a realistic, personalised or complex role where they will be expected to empathise and respond as a specific character perhaps very alien to their own disposition. It is crucial that time, space and appropriate preparation be allowed for this **enrolment** process. This often takes the form of concentration exercises, preliminary improvisation, in-role writing, artwork or physical tasks.

The space needs to be made as congruent as possible with the fictitious situation – in a personalised role-play, it is difficult for participants to respond appropriately as, say, adults in a crisis interview, if there is an external, amused audience, or they are being asked to sit at desks or on the floor. Appropriate time must be made for the action, in order to fully establish concentration and dramatic tension. Dramatic tension, essential to the effective operation of any drama, will only occur if the characters' goals and purposes are strong, their tasks are clear, and the action is delayed by appropriate constraints. All these are crucial.

There are basic skills necessary for participants in any form of drama, including the ability to make and accept the contract and the functions appropriate to the genre; the ability to sustain and take responsibility for shaping dramatic action appropriately; and the ability both to respond and to interact sensitively and appropriately as an actor.

Drama generates its own meanings, most of which cannot be reduced to simplistic resolutions and assumptions or written down as exam answers. However, it is possible, and in some cases necessary, to reflect upon the meanings, both those personal to each participant and those shared by the group. In the case of inexperienced participants this reflective process may need to be carefully structured, and even to begin within the dramatic fiction itself.

Limitations and constraints

Drama and theatre entail a number of limitations and constraints, which spring from the nature of the art form itself and which must be borne in mind when contemplating using drama in the arena of conflict management.

Drama is fictional and voluntary. Even if dealing with 'real-life' events, the dramatist or participant group selects from and adapts those events to construct and manipulate the dramatic narrative *at will*. The drama can only happen with the conscious will and intellectual and emotional commitment of all the participants. For instance, where the conditions for either empathy or distance are not present, the depiction and exploration of conflict through drama become either impossible or spurious.

Drama illustrates, represents, explores and can illuminate conflict, but it is *not* a way of solving real conflict. In real conflicts, the necessary conditions for drama to operate are rarely present. The participants, whether actors or audience, must necessarily agree to suspend their disbelief in order to engage in drama, which the protagonists in conflict are rarely able or willing to do. A characteristic of most real conflicts is that the protagonists won't agree to anything. Drama's participants must be able to empathise with both sides of a question; if the protagonists in a real conflict could empathise with each other they would have de-escalated or abandoned the conflict.

Everybody is at some time or another involved in the heat of a conflict. However, everybody, every student, can also in the right conditions look at the *notion* of conflict quite coolly, and learn about how conflicts happen, and how they might be mediated. That's drama's job – illustrating, representing, exploring and illuminating the underlying principles of conflict, embodied in the fictional conflicts that can be played with and manipulated in drama and theatre. Then the students have a fund of understanding that they might be able to summon to their aid when they are in a real-life conflict, or have to mediate in somebody else's.

Drama in the program

Enhanced forum theatre

As indicated above, the drama techniques used in the program have been mainly improvisational, drawn from the **drama in education** and **theatre of the oppressed** movements. **Process drama**, which is widely used in the classroom, can prove difficult for students and teachers with no experience in drama to master, because there is no 'performance' as such, with clearly defined actors and audience. On the other hand, some of the techniques allow real depth of exploration and understanding of bullying and conflict to occur. **Forum theatre**, the key form of *theatre of the oppressed*, is much easier for everyone to use, as it centres on a play by actors to an audience, whose powers of intervention are limited. However, this can sometimes provide only superficial or unrealistic responses to the conflicts being explored.

Like the whole *Cooling Conflict* program, the drama techniques have gone through a number of phases of experiment and refinement. During the research work, in discussion with participating teachers – both drama-trained and neophytes – at each stage of the project, a clear message came out. *Forum theatre* was simple, clear and safe for the inexperienced to follow. However, *process drama* provided the better and deeper learning, it seemed. Accordingly a new form has been created for the program consisting of the most effective and appropriate elements of both process drama and forum theatre. The result is **enhanced forum theatre**, the central drama strategy of *Cooling Conflict*. The structure and implementation of *enhanced forum theatre* is explained in detail in Chapter 6.

Some drama techniques

Freezing a moment of conflict.

Putting the protagonist in the hot-seat.

Role-circle – enriching the fiction.

Creating a theatrical symbol of conflict.

Forum theatre in action – the spect-actor intervenes.

It starts as traditional forum theatre, where a group of students devise a short play, based on a conflict situation ending in manifest confrontation. However, a number of process drama techniques are then woven into the play to increase its depth. The play is performed twice without stopping so that the audience can grasp the basis of the situation. Then during the third run-through, the audience is invited by the compère or **host** to intervene as **spect-actors**, taking the role of any of the characters involved. The authenticity of their **interventions** is monitored and controlled by the audience, using a convention known as **magic**.

Extension scene

A further extension integrated into the *enhanced forum theatre* framework is the **Scene Four**. This is important to the students' developing understanding of how to handle conflict, because as spect-actors they have been encouraged to intervene directly in scenes of confrontation and passion. This is often the very worst time to try to deal with a conflict, and de-escalation and mediation are often best achieved at another place and another time. This *Scene Four* occurs after the actual forum performance is over and all the *interventions* have been fully explored and discussed. The audience in groups are then asked to identify a character from within the conflict story who might be able to mediate, and an appropriate point in time and place for this to occur. An extension scene is set up, with the actors as before – but perhaps an audience member now taking role as the mediating character. The various groups' suggestions are tried out by the actors, and together with the audience there is further discussion and reflection about which has been most productive in de-escalating or resolving the conflict.

Playbuilding

The first drama experience for all of the students involved in *Cooling Conflicts* apart from the **key class** is the simple but thought-provoking and entertaining one of being spect-actors of a piece of enhanced forum theatre. However, all the students will also get to devise and 'playbuild' their own plays, where they will encounter other process drama techniques and deepen their understanding of the causes and structures of conflict. Some confident teachers (and students) will no doubt experiment further with variations, and more inclusions from process drama and other rehearsal techniques.

Playbuilding entails developing from scratch a group-devised drama, crystallising a theme involving a contentious social issue or a personal story into a specific episode. The students explore the episode to generate a focus question to drive a drama, demanding to know more about who did what, and why, and what was at stake for them. The students then set about devising the actual enhanced forum theatre play based on their group discussions and improvisations. Playbuilding techniques are useful to provide a story and a starting point for the forum theatre work, and a number are included in Chapter 7.

Drama games and activities

Preliminary dramatic games and exercises are often necessary especially with the younger students, focusing them on the drama and encouraging group cohesion and cooperation. These **warm-up** exercises are needed at the beginning of a series of peer teaching experiences, to establish that context of performance and build the trust between the **peer teachers** and their classes. The games have also proved invaluable in the peer teaching classes when the prepared process drama and forum theatre run off the rails, or just run out, giving the peer teachers time to re-group and find the next step to get back on track.

Theatre in education

Cooling Conflicts is centred in the classroom using enhanced forum theatre within the curriculum and down through the year groups. However, after a key or **first relay class** has passed on the baton, they will usually still be committed to the program. If they have time, they may be able to help the younger groups with their own peer teaching, and that is very valuable. It may also be possible to take the students another step – to extend the in-school peer teaching beyond the school walls into the local community with an 'outreach' performance of **theatre in education** (TIE) based on conflict. The group might identify a community group with significant and particular conflict problems, and present them with a piece of theatre that reflects and explores those problems not just theatrically, but in a way that allows for audience interaction. For one key class, for instance, the conflict theme they identified was that of the family problems that arise when young people leave school or home. The target audience were school leavers from a contrasting selection of three schools. Four situations of unresolved conflict were devised, mostly based on the stories garnered from the audience-to-be. These were woven together using the familiar metaphorical frame of a game-show. To bring in the audience, the team used a version of enhanced forum theatre. The production, *As One Door Closes*, satisfied both the audiences and the key class.

The techniques of playbuilding, drama exercises and theatre in education are described in detail in Chapter 7.

Peer teaching

The use of **peer teaching** to enhance learning is an established practice that has been used extensively particularly in primary schools, in the field of sports coaching, and in a range of other formal and informal learning environments.[4] Although peer teaching can involve students of the same age teaching each other, or even younger peers instructing older students, the most common and successful application in schools has involved older peers teaching younger students. Most peer teaching involves single students teaching one-on-one, or a small group of learners. Students or groups of students teaching whole classes are comparatively infrequent.

There has been a large number of recent studies into the effectiveness of peer teaching in schools as educators search for more effective ways of engaging students in their learning. All these studies have found clear and convincing proof that peer teaching can be an extremely effective tool for improving learning in the classroom. Peer teaching has been shown to be valuable in a wide variety of subject areas and teaching environments, and four major educational benefits have been identified as apparent in all these settings.[5] Every one of these four educational benefits were clearly identified in trials of the *Cooling Conflict* program at all stages of the research.

1. Students' learning is maximised when they are able to apply what they have learned in meaningful ways to new contexts.[6] We found that peer teaching younger classes about conflict management through drama produced much clearer and more sophisticated understandings of the *Cooling Conflict* program in the peer teachers in every case. Whilst they were being taught, the key and first relay classes increasingly demonstrated an understanding of conflict management through drama, but it was usually only when they taught their younger peers that they really grasped the concepts of **mediation** and **de-escalation** and began to apply these in their own lives.

2. The most conducive environment for learning is an interactive and cooperative one, characterised by dialogue.[7] This was particularly evident when first relay class Year 8 and 9 students were working with the key class students. The interactions between the peer teachers and students reflected high levels of cooperation and enthusiasm and clearly operated as dialogues. Every single first relay class student who has been involved in the program has identified the peer teaching by the senior drama class as one of the highlights of the experience, because they felt they could identify with their peer teachers and because the learning relationship was cooperative and interactive.

3. Students learn more in a secure, cooperative classroom atmosphere where they take

responsibility for their learning.[8] Forming groups to plan and peer teach clearly empowered the *key* and *relay* students, allowing them to work cooperatively and giving them a sense of ownership of their work. Drama is by its nature a student-centred and cooperative enterprise, and when this is linked to the positive mentoring provided by peer teaching, the classroom atmosphere becomes highly supportive and empowering for the students.

4. When students take responsibility for their own learning, and use innovative methods to do so, motivation is higher and learning more sustained.[9] Student responses to the questionnaires strongly identify very high levels of motivation in the *Cooling Conflict* program, and significant persistence of learning about conflict management. The key class students were initially nervous about teaching younger classes, but by the end of the process they had greatly enjoyed the experience and devoted significant amounts of time and energy to it. A number of the students emerged as natural teachers. Interestingly, in each trial of *Cooling Conflict*, a few key class students who had been least committed and active in learning about conflict management became the most enthusiastic and active in the teaching of it. The same has been true of the early relay classes, and in particular cases, indigenous students who had been very quiet and passive during the learning phase emerged as natural leaders and teachers, when working with groups of primary school students.

Empowering the peer teachers

Some recent research to examine the benefits of peer teaching for those doing the teaching was conducted in 1998[10] and the results indicate that peer teaching increases both social and intellectual awareness. The peer teachers also showed significant gains in empathy, and were more clearly able to recognise that they could change habitual patterns of behaviour. Finally, this research also showed that peer teaching empowered the students, increasing their sense of mastery and self-esteem. The authors of the study concluded: '. . . it would be hard to think of another method that would enable so much intellectual, social and personal growth'.[11]

The social and personal benefits of peer teaching are particularly significant in bullying management. Research has shown that that peer teaching enhances the self-confidence and self-esteem of students who have been peer tutors.[12] This is obviously of benefit to students who are being bullied and who lack confidence and the ability to assert themselves. However, a recent study in the UK also indicated that peer teaching improved the self-image and behaviour of disruptive and difficult students identified as 'negative leaders'. As a result of peer teaching, the aggression and high-risk behaviour demonstrated by these students disappeared.[13]

These findings have been clearly confirmed in the program. Over half of the key and relay class peer teachers reported that they actually applied what they had learned to conflicts in their own lives, and very many did so successfully. Almost every student response to the questionnaires has identified the program as valuable in terms of learning about conflict and feeling empowered to apply this learning. This is an exciting connection with recent research on bullying behaviour in Canada that has identified that usually most of the bystanders to bullying (about 70% in the episodes studied) take no pleasure in the bullying, 25% try to intervene, and many more of the rest would like to if they dared.[14] Not only does *Cooling Conflict* give student bystanders a broader range of strategies for intervention and mediation, but the change in the ethos and ambience of the school will support positive intervention more readily, as all parties – bully, bullied and bystanders – are more aware of conflict and bullying, and how to deal with it.

The later relay class students in the primary schools surveyed during the program have responded in precisely the same way. They overwhelmingly identify the experience of being taught by Year 8 and 9 high school students as extremely enjoyable and exciting. Almost without exception they also state that they learned effectively about conflict management from the older students. An added outcome for the upper primary relay classes was the opportunity to visit their local high schools and to do the *Cooling Conflict* program there. The teachers and students from these primary classes noted how exciting this was for them, giving them a sense of belonging and helping to de-mystify the high schools concerned. In more than one school cluster, the administration has incorporated *Cooling Conflict* as part of the regular induction program for the primary students.

Empowering the learners

Other recent research has focused on the effects of peer teaching on the students being taught.[15] This research has produced clear evidence that teenagers learn more effectively from their peers than from traditional, teacher-centred instruction. One study found that this was particularly evident with students with low academic achievement and learning difficulties. Whilst the students in the study being peer taught showed much higher levels of literacy and comprehension, there was no significant difference in classroom behaviour between them and the students receiving teacher-centred instruction.[16]

Again, the *Cooling Conflict* program has confirmed these findings. Despite their inexperience in teaching younger classes, the key class peer teachers are invariably extremely successful in teaching about conflict management and in helping the relay class students to prepare their own teaching. At the same time, the key class groups are able to exercise a high level of positive classroom management, and this is because the relay class students have all been strongly motivated to cooperate with their key class peer teachers and to learn from them. This motivation to learn and the positive behaviour management which goes with it is apparent at the level of Year 8 and 9 relay class students teaching large groups of primary students at induction days at high schools. Although they are untrained in classroom management skills, the relay class students are successfully able to teach the program because of their commitment to it, and because the Year 6 and 7 students they are teaching are enthusiastic and strongly motivated by the structure of the program. In turn, the students from primary relay classes clearly confirm in interviews and questionnaires that their first relay peer teachers have been successful in their teaching. They particularly identify the enthusiasm and enjoyment that was generated by the peer teaching. The first relay students are fully aware of this response, and acknowledge it as crucial in the increased self-esteem generated by the program.

A word about peer mediation

Despite clear evidence that peer teaching is extremely effective in both enhancing learning and empowering students, it has been a neglected resource in the field of bullying and conflict management. In particular, there is little evidence apart from *Cooling Conflict* in the current literature on bullying and conflict in schools nationally or internationally that peer teaching has been used as a tool to address conflict or bullying. Instead, the use of school students as **peer mediators** has become widespread in recent years due to increasing concern with conflict in schools. Programs using *peer mediation* are most common in primary schools both in Australia and overseas; in most cases upper primary or secondary students are trained in simple mediation techniques and then encouraged to act as mediators outside the classroom.

However, a major review of nine peer mediation programs carried out in four states in the United States questioned the validity of peer mediation as an effective strategy to deal with conflict and bullying.[17] Whilst reported incidents of conflict declined in some of the primary schools, there was limited evidence to show that the students of the schools had actually learned to manage their conflicts better, or that conflicts were genuinely de-escalated by the peer mediators. In most of the high schools involved in the review, conflict had not reduced at all; in some it had apparently increased.

A meta-evaluation of the bullying management programs implemented in a number of different countries was carried out in 2002 by Ken Rigby for the Attorney-General's Department here in Australia.[18] This report reached the conclusion that none of the bullying management programs tried in these countries over the past decade, including peer mediation, had made any significant difference to bullying in schools. The American experience, Rigby's meta-evaluation and the *Cooling Conflict* research all suggest that students, especially secondary school students, are far more likely to become competent at managing conflicts in their own lives if they empowered to do so by learning about conflict management and then teaching what they have learned to their peers.

More important than that, even, is the effect on the school as a whole. We constantly find that students who have peer taught younger students are no longer inclined to bully them, and the first steps to effecting real change in the atmosphere and network of relationships within schools has been taken. It stands to reason that the warm and friendly relationships established between older and younger students through the prolonged and pleasurable contact in the drama class will dismantle the perceptions of 'difference', create positive power relationships based on respect and caring, and begin to establish informal 'buddying' systems, particularly between the lower secondary and upper primary students (the very ages when bullying is statistically most likely to occur).

Notes

1. Boal, A. (1979) *Theatre of the Oppressed.* London: Pluto Press.
2. E.g. Heathcote, D. & Bolton, G. (1995) *Drama for Learning: Dorothy Heathcote's Mantle of the Expert Approach to Education.* Portsmouth, NH: Heinemann.
3. Vygotski, L. (1933) Play and its Role in the Mental Development of the Child, in Bruner, J. et al. (1974) *Play: a Reader.* London: Penguin, p. 548.
4. Billson, J. & Tiberius, R. (1991) Effective Social Arrangements for Teaching and Learning. *New Directions for Teaching and Learning,* no. 45, Spring.
5. Svinicki, M. (1991) Practical Implications of Cognitive Theories. *New Directions for Teaching and Learning,* no. 45, p. 30.
6. Ibid., p. 30.
7. Billson, J. & Tiberius, R. op. cit., p. 93.
8. Forsyth, I. (1999) *Delivering a Course: Practical Strategies for Teachers, Lecturers and Trainers.* London: Kogan Page.
9. Ibid., p. 63.

10. Rubin, J. & Herbert, M. (1998) Peer Teaching – Model for Active Learning. *College Teaching,* Winter, vol. 48, no. 1.
11. Ibid., p. 14.
12. Simmons, D. et al. (1995) Effects of Explicit Teaching and Peer Tutoring on the Reading Achievement of Learning-Disabled and Low-Performing Students in Regular Classrooms. *The Elementary School Journal,* 95, no. 5.
13. Morrison, M. (2004) Risk and Responsibility: The Potential of Peer Teaching to Address Negative Leadership. Cambridge, UK: unpublished article.
14. Craig, W. & Pepler, D. (2000) Observations of Bullying and Victimization in the Schoolyard, in Wendy Craig (ed.) *Childhood Social Development : The Essential Readings.* Malden, MA: Blackwell, pp. 126–8.
15. Simmons, D. et al. (1995) op. cit.
16. Goodlad, S. & Hirst, B. (1989) *Peer Tutoring: A Guide to Learning by Teaching.* London: Kogan Page.
17. Powell, K. et al. (1994) A Review of Selected School-Based Conflict Resolution and Peer Mediation Projects. *Journal of Social Health,* Dec. 1995, vol. 65, no. 10.
18. Rigby, K. (2002) *A Meta-Evaluation of Methods and Approaches to Reducing Bullying in Pre-Schools and Early Primary School in Australia.* Canberra: Commonwealth Attorney-General.

The story so far

What the students learn and what they make of it

Cooling Conflict has developed over the years through listening to the students' responses. This chapter uses the words of some of the students and their teachers in the research schools to reveal what they have learnt as a result of their involvement, and more importantly the extent to which they apply what they have learnt to real-life situations.

What the students learn about conflict

A basic premise of the program is that effective conflict management is dependent on conflict understanding. During the research, a number of drama techniques were tried out. Some were more productive than others in eventually generating the ability to manage conflict, but there were significant gains in conflict *understanding* at all schools. Virtually every student ended up able to identify and define the three stages of conflict – latent, emergent and manifest – as a Year 11 student put it, articulately and succinctly:

> *. . . The way this is done is by firstly learning to see conflict emerging, how it grows and then how it gets really serious. The same three stages can always be identified. The first stage is latent conflict. This means the conditions are there for trouble but not obvious. The second stage is emerging – when something happens, or begin to see trouble. Manifest is when both sides know they are in conflict with each other and every one can see the same thing.*

This level of understanding reached right down to the lower primary level, and more surprisingly, informants of varying ages across the schools could remember the three stages a year later. Even for those who used the terminology only superficially, the meaning behind the words was important. For many students, this new terminology promoted their elevated status, importance and knowledge to others – adults included. Some students even developed useful metaphors to assist their younger peers to visualise the conflict process:

There are three stages of conflict: you've got latent, emerging and manifest. Say, you've got a pot: the water's cold – that's latent. Emerging is when it's bubbling, and manifest, which is the next stage, is when it's overflowing.

Latent is where the sticks are in the pile. Emerging is where the very first spark is lit, and manifest is the very peak of the whole fire.

The students' comprehension was fully realised only after significant reflection. One year after the program had been conducted in her school, and using a real life conflict as an exemplar, Emily noted how her ability to analyse conflict had increased over time (in her school, the term 'brewing' was used for the 'emerging' phase):

. . . we were getting into a squabbly stage and we know it's just because it's the conflict brewing – it's brewing over – it's really weird, but I understand why people fight and how it can be solved . . .

Her use of the term 'conflict brewing' was consciously considered. When asked, Emily claimed that actual terms do not go through her head; rather the meaning behind them does: 'I just think, well we're in the early stages, it's not over, we can save this, you know . . . I think it can make it a lot easier that way'. In fact so essential did the students in her class consider this information that several claimed they 'found the three stages of conflict to be the most useful aspect of the project, in terms of what I learnt'. Others were emphatic that 'the knowledge of conflict is always going to stay. That is so useful to have'.

As students' level of comprehension increases, the appropriateness of their response to problems improves, so they can clearly distinguish the need to move beyond immediate conflict to reflection: 'It sorta changed my attitude about conflict. It made me think ahead of my conflict before going in and doing more damage'.

The transfer of learning into life contexts

The overwhelming anecdotal evidence of students and teachers confirms that valuable, usable learning happens. However, we can justifiably question the extent to which these gains are a result of the program, and how accurately this can be measured. Moreover, how do we gauge students' understanding of the principles of conflict as they apply not just to familiar situations involving family members and friends, but also citizens on a national and global level? Drama scholars like Steve Cockett[1] question how we can know for sure the effect of discoveries facilitated through drama, and points out 'even Boal admits there is no proper instrument for measuring the effectiveness of his techniques'. The relationship between students, learning and empowerment is very complex, as splendidly uncertain as drama itself. As the researchers grappled with these issues, we frequently envisaged the ripple effect upon the water's surface of a stone thrown in a pool. The ripple cannot be measured, nor can all its effects above and beneath the water be calculated, yet it patently exists. In the same way, for most of the students involved in the study, meaningful learning will in some form or another stay with them.

What we can do is listen carefully to students' own accounts, observe their behaviour, and make informed inferences. Education is a lifelong process, where students continue to learn and make connections themselves, as a teacher comments:

> *I mean, it might sound like an exaggeration but . . . you would imagine that for some kids . . .* Cooling Conflict *was the most positive educational experience they've ever had . . . Whatever happens, they'll take with them this experience . . .* Cooling Conflict *was an example of where they showed that they could contribute to the total product . . .*

In fact one student, who had been very disillusioned with school, claimed that if it wasn't for the connection she made to the program 'I would have been out of here by now'.

According to one Principal, his school has adopted several strategies, supported by the entire school, which aim to assist students both *in* conflict and *about* conflict. *Cooling Conflict* facilitated this whole-school approach, which the students were then able to transfer to the wider context of their lives:

> *Kids tend to do things the way their parents did and . . . I think that's the stuff that these kids are missing out on because the relationships are breaking down fairly regularly. People deal with broken relationship stuff in terms of either violence or avoidance. They move or they expect somebody else to fix it. Often they come up here and we're trying to help them sort out a feud between this neighbour and that neighbour because that's impacting at school. But to me* Cooling Conflict *gives a simple language and a process that the kids can work their way through and they can give it a go in their own lives.*

A Year 9 student agrees:

> *Yep. Instead of yelling at each other they talk through it and that, and try and work out their problems. The people that were doing the project they sort of don't got into fights as much as what they did before they started it.*

Visits made by the researchers after a substantial period of time continue to confirm this pattern of approval, with the clear finding that the students feel strongly they are acquiring knowledge useful to their personal lives. Additionally, students perceive *Cooling Conflict* as a catalyst for facilitating the conscious decision to modify their conduct, to the extent that they are often able to avoid becoming involved in conflict: 'I do think a lot [about the repercussions of my actions] now, because I've settled a lot since the project'. This student attributed his improved relationship with teachers directly to the program:

> All the teachers say 'you've changed a lot since last year and we don't want that to blow out the window'. . . . With conflict, I used to – if somebody said something to me, no ifs or buts I'd be straight into them, rearing them up – but now I either just leave it or I just go and ask them 'Hey, did you say this?' and if they say 'No', I just leave them alone.

In addition to improving their conduct with their peers, many students spoke of better and more empathic relationships with their teachers; a direct result of having been placed in their shoes:

> [Being a peer teacher] gave me a bit of experience . . . finding out what it was really like for other people, like teachers . . . see what they go through in a lesson and that. I sort of wanted to be a teacher before the program showed me what it was really like! I'm normally used to being the smart arse, being rude to the teacher and that. It's a bit different when it's turned around on you . . . it's sort of made me stop doing it.

Significantly, students perceive *Cooling Conflict* to be just as important as existing curriculum content, if not more so. Additionally, the attitude of the majority of their parents ensures the program is widely endorsed. Such is the support that several parents, having recognised the potential benefits the program could afford their children, have taken on the role of allies, coercing and encouraging their initially reluctant children to participate. 'Because I'm always in trouble at school and that, Dad thought it would be good for me to keep going with the program . . . because it might help me with the problems with my teachers and that.'

It seems clear that the students' families are also beneficiaries of the ripples. Interestingly, several students measured their success by using their parents as gauges: '[The program] worked so many times on my Mum and Dad'. For another, *Cooling Conflict* provided him with the opportunity to be able to truthfully 'tell Mum and Dad I'm learning' for the first time.

Students also apply what they have learnt directly to their own family lives, as well as to the family/school relationship. As a Year 11 student articulately puts it: 'I've started to define conflict better for myself at home and in school. I can see something happening and say "hey that's a latent conflict – look out" or "we're into a manifest conflict – better butt out of this"'. Another Year 11 student said: 'Yeah, if I know there's going to be an argument with my Mum I'll just walk off and I'll just think of a few things to say and then I'll come back with a few different points I can say instead of my bad temper'.

Even sibling rivalry can be de-escalated – as the same student also said:

> I've talked to my sister about it. I was using some techniques on her and asking her if it would help – she was very helpful in that way so she even understands a little bit of it too. Just by me understanding what I do to create conflict, that has stopped a lot of fighting at home.

The students know that what they have learned is no panacea for all conflicts, of course, and what they have learned helps them to be frank about the program's limitations:

> Yes, I've got more out of it in real life. My parents are talking about separation – it's a bit tense in our house at times. So I've started thinking 'there's trouble brewing' and I've started using the words in the house. I said to Mum: 'You've got some trouble brewing', or 'latent conflict'. [Interviewer: Did she understand?] I don't think she knew what I was talking about! [Interviewer: Did it have any effect?] I didn't see any – it was too tense!

Mary, a senior girl, had been involved in serious conflict with her mother and had left home for a short period. In interview, she explained how she had returned to the family home and used conflict management to diffuse conflict with her mother. In particular, she described how she used to 'forum' her behaviour in her own mind to decide how to deal with issues of conflict. She would also point out to her mother when their conflict was moving from emerging to manifest. 'I would go home and if we would fight I'd say "Look now . . . Mum – I know you're angry – I know you're feeling anger" and she'd say "What did they teach you at school!?"' Whilst Mary credits the program as being a 'lifesaver' for herself and her mother, she simultaneously acknowledges that it was so on a complementary level:

Interviewer:	*Be really honest here. The stuff we did is worthwhile?*
Mary:	*It's been a lifesaver . . .*
Interviewer:	*You spoke about a new honesty that will stay with you. Is this a result of what you did over the two years?*
Mary:	*Not completely – it was on the way anyhow, but more thoroughly and effectively because the idea of latent conflict was in the back of my mind. It refined my knowledge of how to deal with the conflict. I would have been able to do it anyway, but probably not as fast or as effectively. As an aid it enhanced the relationship – enhanced the way I dealt with conflict.*

One of the most exciting aspects of the program, that schools notice when they implement it, is that students identified as troublemakers or otherwise disaffected in their normal schooling often emerge as the natural leaders and the most committed participants. Tracey, a Year 8 girl, was violent and uncontrollable, performing very poorly in her studies, a grim joke among the teachers, none of whom could control her. One of them put it frankly in the program's in-service: 'She's the school's worst student – you wait till you meet her'. She was under threat of expulsion, along with her best friend Elaine, another troubled and violent student. From the first moment the Year 11 students arrived to peer teach their class, they threw themselves into the drama – which gave their frustrated energy and impulsive imaginativeness scope – and led from the front, especially when it came to peer teaching primary students. At the end of the program, both had changed, and both had had the threats of expulsion lifted. The teachers marvelled. We decided to follow Tracey, and see if this was just a flash in the pan. We finish this chapter with the full and moving story of Tracey. Two years later, we closely observed almost the same effect on a student with a very similar profile – and coincidentally the same forename (which of course wasn't Tracey)!

Both these students took leadership roles in the drama work, where they showed flair, and in the peer teaching. More surprisingly to us, some of the leaders in the peer teaching are students who have been apparently very passive or even resistant to the drama work. Two Year 11 students when first interviewed showed hostility to their schooling in general and their drama teacher in particular, and announced that they would not be taking part in the project, as they were intending 'to be out of here before it happens'. Though their participation was severely affected by absenteeism and their deteriorating relationship with the drama teacher, who made no secret that she had little time for them, somehow they had learned enough to turn up on the day of the peer teaching, and confidently and articulately led the whole session. Both are shown on the teachers' training video, accurately explaining the concepts and skilfully leading the drama work – and both subsequently stayed on to complete their Senior school-leaving examination, ascribing this explicitly to the project, and to take a mentoring role in the program the following year.

Some of the richest inferences can be made indirectly from anecdotal evidence, especially when so much of it is corroborative. Recently, one of the teachers who has been running a changing and developing version of the program for some years now, recounted with amusement, but just a touch of awe, an incident that had happened that morning. A Year 8 student ran into her staffroom calling out 'Miss, Miss, there's a conflict down by the swimming pool'. This boy had previously met the teacher three years earlier when she escorted the secondary peer teachers to his primary year 5 class. She had had little contact with him since he arrived in the high school, and he had not been involved in the program in the interim. When she scrambled to her feet to go and check this situation out, he immediately reacted soothingly with 'There's no hurry Miss, it's not got to manifest yet – it's just emerging'. She rightly recognised that this was not only an example of the student using the terminology correctly after three years, but using it confidently to make an informed judgment about action to de-escalate conflict, and proffer mature advice to an adult.

Other cognitive, personal and social learning

Stan and Alexia were two Aboriginal Year 9 students in the same class. When the Year 11 students came to their Aboriginal Studies class to do the peer teaching, they initially responded quite differently. Stan, an extrovert and normally disruptive student, behaved like those students described above – by throwing himself in the program and the drama, and leading from the front throughout. Alexia, a slight, timid girl, sat totally silent through the Year 11 teaching, eyes downcast, reluctant to participate or even move. She was just as passive and silent throughout the planning and preparation for their own peer teaching, and was consigned to sit at the side and observe her bolder classmates.

On the day of the peer teaching, a transformation occurred in Alexia's behaviour. The primary class was too big (46 students), and very boisterous. Jim, a brash and rather over-confident classmate, made the mistake of over-exciting a group of ten very big and energetic Year 6 students who then ran out of control, becoming quite naughty. The teacher was about to rescue Jim when Alexia rose, walked over to the group, dispatched Jim unceremoniously to the sidelines with a toss of her head, quietened the rest of the room with another, and calmly took immediate charge of the younger children, who towered over her, but became like lambs in her hands as she quietly and surely got them back on task, taught them for 15 minutes, and then handed them back to her astonished colleagues.

After these experiences, Stan was highly articulate about what the program had done for him. Alexia on the other hand could really offer little explanation of why she had intervened other than 'Well, I thought the day was pretty cool, how I handled it – I dunno – I just said it – it just came natural'. Six months later, however, she was surer of one outcome of the program:

> I thought it helped me because all last year me and my dad we fighted a lot and like we'd get into arguments and stuff, but after the Cooling Conflict I just realised that everything was – it was cool after that. It helped.

That term she also surprised her teacher again:

Alexia auditioned for the musical! That's a huge outcome for her – she didn't even go to the musical we had the previous time, even though the main roles were for Aboriginal kids. She just turned up to audition. She was really confident, and I've never seen her present like that before. She's usually totally quiet and shy . . . I think it's got a lot to do with the drama experience they had through Cooling Conflict.

Change in attitude amongst students is not confined solely to diminished levels of conflict and improved ability to understand and manage them appropriately, but to increased confidence and self-esteem also, strikingly illustrated by a student's observations of her peers:

They're not afraid to perform in front of the class anymore. The boys are still a bit immature and can't concentrate as much as we'd prefer them to . . . but in other classes . . . the embarrassment was overcome. [One boy] would never even say 'boo!' in other classes and then he had to get up for a speech in Science and he was really loud and the teachers were exclaiming, 'Wow! What's wrong with him!?' . . . That was through Drama, so what we learnt shows up in other subjects.

In that school, a significant proportion of students in the program chose to enrol in the subject Drama the following year. Both they and their teachers acknowledged this outcome as being directly linked to the sense of empowerment engendered by *Cooling Conflict*, as well as an attempt to recreate and sustain it:

Interviewer: *Do you think that those kids choosing to enrol in Drama in Year 9 could be attributed in any way to their involvement in the Project?*

Teacher: *Oh definitely, yeah, yeah. I think they saw Drama as a positive subject and something they could perform in or something they could achieve in.*

One finding that did clearly emerge from the research is that participants understand they have a choice in how they manage and approach conflict situations:

Whether you intend it or not . . . some of the ways of looking at life and doing things are going to rub off, and it's not just one way of doing something . . . I have a choice of doing it my way or all these other ways . . .

Building on this, socialisation is another strong theme to emerge across all schools as a direct result of the peer teaching. This is because teaching is essentially a social activity, through which social skills are refined and enhanced. Unfortunately, traditional schooling patterns especially in secondary schools make it difficult for teachers to create much social interaction amongst students of different ages, and the hierarchy of the school playground means that students from different groups do not often interact. They themselves are well aware of this, and it is one of the reasons they look forward to the peer teaching:

[Peer teaching will provide us with a greater insight] into them as we'll be able to see more of them than we normally would in the playground and stuff . . . We'll be able to go 'Oh, I know that person. Like I did that drama thing' or whatever. Might build, like, better relationships between the youngies and the oldies.

'Fitting in' and being accepted by one's peers is essential to foster positive self-esteem. For students new to a school, 'clique stratification' is a matter of immediate concern as they have to establish a niche for themselves – a task made especially harder where there is cultural difference. Hassem, an immigrant student, explains:

When I arrived at the school . . . on top of getting into the whole program . . . I needed to estab-lish something with my peers. And because I had no affiliation with any of the younger stu-dents we would be teaching, I had to establish something with them also . . . I've got to admit, initially I wasn't too keen on the whole situation. Nevertheless, [the relay class students] walked away from the peer teaching and they greeted me differently afterwards . . . There was a different level of understanding between me and them. So previously I think I had some conflict with some of them because of my appearance and so on. I mean, I don't see anything different about myself but obviously other people do. That's just something that I've gotten used to but, yeah, I think it was productive.

Ella, one of Hassem's classmates, had also been unhappy with the amount of cultural conflict at school. 'Before [the program] there were so many conflicts because I've got a foreign back-ground and everything and they'd say all these names and stuff to me.' Previously, she would either 'ignore it' or 'say stuff back'. However following the completion of the program, Ella noted that 'ever since that happened actually – you just made me realise it – it doesn't happen anymore . . . it never happens, they've all forgotten it'.

Many students claim to have a clearer understanding of cultural conflict – despite the fact that this component is not given an explicit focus. Such positive attitudinal change highlights a new tolerance: '[The program] taught me that it is only different colours of skin, but we're all the same people, we all have feelings'.

Staff members from a school in rural NSW, with a history of tension and disharmony in the community, also noted the increased level of cultural harmony within the school and its positive impact on the wider community:

The whole tone of the school's been improving . . . and I think [the program] would have contributed to that . . . Number one, with the kids getting this positive sense of themselves, number two, positive publicity out in the community, and how we are perceived because originally, when I came to this school, it was perceived as the most racist high school in Australia. And to be running an innovative program that looks at conflict resolution through Drama turns that attitude around, not only in the community but amongst our kids and our parents. We are taking positive steps to change, and I think that's really important.

The experiences and the voices of the student (and teacher) participants portrayed on these pages clearly indicate that the program can be of benefit to schoolchildren everywhere. It is also evident that alongside these 'ordinary' successes are individual cases of transformational change, which see some students make exceptional advances – such as Tracey whose involvement personifies the transformational nature of *Cooling Conflict*.

What the students learned in culture, drama and curriculum

I can truthfully tell Mum and Dad I'm learning, for the first time.

The students bring their own cultural agendas into the drama work, which then flows out into the resulting general understandings, sometimes benevolently, sometimes more ambivalently. Many of the conflicts explored throughout this program have cultural implications, in a broader or narrower sense. One consistent principle related to the oblique way dramatic learning operates is that the conflicts explored can arise directly or indirectly from the students' experience and ideas. However, these issues are deliberately not privileged, but fictionalised and then dealt with as they emerge, as part of the 'natural order of conflict'.

An exceptional example of this phenomenon occurred during a theatre in education project inspired by the program, which also used a form of **forum theatre**. For those students who are wary of disclosing information to others, and preferred to deal with conflict internally, the interactive drama helps them to overcome their fear of disclosure, by exploiting the **protection** of role that forum theatre provides. It is through the creation of one's own fictional world that we are able to understand and change the real one. This process occurs both as a requirement and a result of identifying with a particular role.

I just wanted to see the conflict [depicted in the forum] resolved . . . because I had the same conflict. I wanted to see what the outcome would be, what people would suggest, just to help myself.

For this student, the theatre in education was a kind of 'rehearsal for life'. Through such embodied representations students are able to both think and feel as another person, and relate that to their own experience.

For many students, the opportunity to learn in ways other than traditional formats is liberating. As one of the students aptly states, 'With drama, you can actually express your feelings', and another 'they taught me a lot of things that I didn't already know . . . and you don't have to be stuck in the classroom on a chair being real quiet and that, you can actually get up'.

Since conflict is so endemic to drama, drama work itself reinforces that conflict is a natural, even healthy part of life that often serves to draw our attention to issues that need addressing. As they learn more skills taking roles in drama, students can recognise more clearly that fear and dislike of conflict is frequently unfounded, and that conflict can actually strengthen relations between people:

Conflict isn't always a bad thing . . . the manifest stage just clearly displays that people can't always hold things in . . . conflict happening brings you closer once more to the person. You realise that once you have gone through that you can still maintain a friendship.

The outcome hinges upon how individuals respond to conflict, and in particular, their ability to consider perspectives other than their own. Whilst it is

easier to run away in the short term . . . if you want a long term resolution that's going to stay fixed, then you've got to compromise, you've got to talk about it, you've got to work at it until it's resolved to everyone's satisfaction.

The story of Tracey

Tracey was a 13-year-old student who, like many others, was targeted for involvement in the program by her teachers, due to her reputation as a severe behaviour problem. Tracey's parents are no longer together and she resides in a low socio-economic area of the community – already known for its history of racial disharmony – where the residents also struggle with difficulties such as violence and alcoholism. On some occasions Tracey drew inspiration from events that occurred in her street and local community when developing conflict scenarios during forum theatre workshops:

Interviewer: *Is that something that has happened before in your neighbourhood?*

Tracey: *Ages ago when I first moved here yes, but it has quieted down recently up here and it's . . . There used to be violence a lot up there . . . Beer bottles smashed every night, violence and verbal abuse, and men bashing women.*

Tracey was fatalistic about her environment, stating that there was 'no point worrying about it'. Whilst she did admit to being fearful about what could happen to her, she felt that there was 'not much I can do about it. If they hit me, I stand back up. I don't care'. Nevertheless we sensed that underneath this bravado cowered a very frightened girl, but one with a very strong moral sense. She also stated that she wasn't scared, but felt 'really bad when they hit women and that', and went on to describe that at such times she wanted to 'jump out of her bedroom window' to intervene.

The beginning

Tracey's early perceptions of the study were typical of many participants, in that she 'thought it would be just so cool to get out of class and bludge for a period'. Tracey's decision not to take the program too seriously, to 'just hand [the consent form] in and see how it goes', was born partly out of her belief that the program would be a waste of time, and partly through fear of drama. As for many of the other students, *Cooling Conflict* was Tracey's first real experience of drama. However her mother Eva was able to recognise positive changes in her behaviour: 'Well she was in a terrible lot of trouble and she just needed a way out I think, and drama gave her that way out where she could express her feelings'. As Tracey began to overcome her feelings of shame and reluctance to participate, her attitude towards the program also started to change: '. . . I never thought drama was my type, but now I think it's really useful and helpful . . . it turned out pretty cool . . . I like it actually'. Tracey started sharing her experiences with her mother. 'She used to come home and she'd say she's in this drama and that she liked it and you could see her face, just the change in her face when she'd talk about it.'

Tracey's growing realisation that *Cooling Conflict* offered her new, constructive ways of dealing with conflict meant that her engagement and commitment to the program's success also grew. This was evident in her attempts to find more positive ways to deal with conflict, which she practised during several pieces of forum theatre:

> *I liked Forum Theatre. It was pretty good. Because, like, if you have a different idea you can put it in and most of the things that we're doing are real life situations and then we can deal with them and know how to handle them because a real life situation comes up like that.*

Leader of the pack

Tracey's commitment to the program and her peer teachers had a positive effect on many of her classmates who often looked to her for direction. This result was not lost on her peer teachers: 'Tracey cracked everyone up. She was really good with the kids and I think she helped everyone boost their confidence because she was involved in everything and encouraged kids to be involved too'.

Being able to work with students from different year levels was one of the most valuable aspects of the program for Tracey:

Interviewer: *What would you say was the most worthwhile and valuable aspect of the project for you personally?*

Tracey: *Working with other people from the group and getting to know them more and working with older people and younger and teaching the skills we had learnt . . . I liked having the opportunity to try and teach them and socialise with other people and work with other people from the new group and the co-workers we had, like from the Year 11 key class last year, how they used to come in, we got to know them . . .*

An emerging awareness of self

Tracey's engagement in the study was coupled with an increasing awareness of self, not just as a leader, but in overall behaviour as well. Such success was further tempered by a reflection on how her past approaches to conflict management were being gradually replaced by new methods: 'I used to be really violent . . . Like, I'd fight a lot to solve all my problems, but that wasn't the best thing to do . . . it just makes it worse. Now I try and talk about it and if that doesn't work I just leave it'. Whilst these types of comments are promising, and demonstrated Tracey's attempts to de-escalate a conflict situation by walking away from it, at this relatively early stage of the program it was not surprising to discover that she was still clinging on to some of her old habits. Although she was trying to refrain from using violence, Tracey felt that violence was acceptable as long as she did not instigate it:

If they hit me first then I feel that I have every right to hit 'em back. But as long as I don't start the fight and I keep my mouth shut, if someone hits me first, I've got every right to hit 'em back. That's the way I feel.

Aggressive approaches to conflict management become ingrained at an early age for students like Tracey. Thus, the process of learning how to communicate more openly and effectively in conjunction with the realisation that violence is not the only option acts as a source of liberation. Initially Tracey used violence as a means of making herself stronger, and invincible:

Interviewer:	*Would you say that you're coping better with your conflicts now?*
Tracey:	*Oh yeah, for sure. I used to always use violence with my conflicts. Now I haven't been in a fight for ages.*
Interviewer:	*Why did you always use violence?*
Tracey:	*I don't know. I thought it made you a better person.*
Interviewer:	*Violence made you a better person?*
Tracey:	*Yeah, like, I don't know . . . And everyone else . . . It's just the town, I think. The town just thrives on violence.*

Later approaches to conflict management

Although *Cooling Conflict* aims to equip students with skills to assist them in appropriately handling their conflicts, it is unrealistic to expect individuals to remain free from conflict. So we were neither surprised nor alarmed to discover that Tracey was involved in a conflict during a visit to the school six months after the program's completion, but observed intently how she was dealing with the conflict, which had rapidly escalated to the manifest stage. In the past Tracey would have responded aggressively without consideration for the consequences, but we witnessed a move away from such instinctive behaviour. Tracey's attempts to remain calm and rational, to think before she acted, were reflective of her desire to maintain the profound effects the program has had on all areas of her life. This includes her growing confidence and self-esteem, the positive experience school has become and her improved relations with teachers, friends and family members. At the time of this new conflict, she was no longer on report, and her teachers spoke warmly of her continued improvement.

For Tracey, the key lay in her growing ability to stop and consider the consequences of her actions instead of rushing in and regretting the repercussions later on:

I used to get angry and use violence all the time when I was angry but now I just go for walks or take deep breaths, talk it through with my mum or who I'm angry with and just stop and think of the consequences . . . I'm thinking why, always know now to stop and think first. I don't think about latent, emergent and manifest and that. I stop and think of my consequences, then I do what I think is right . . . And then you think, 'Yeah, latent, emergent . . . it only got to emergent', you know, because you then step in . . . The actual words don't go through my head but the stages do, like . . . I usually just think back [to the peer teaching], picture the room in there and everything moving, talking about it, just think about that.

Tracey's initial response to this new conflict was to avoid the situation. She was painfully aware of the fact that any involvement in adverse circumstances would still have dire consequences for her schooling career: 'I'm worried because I'm on my last warning and if I get expelled once more I'm expelled from every school in New South Wales . . .' Tracey retained her sensible approach, and, upon realising that she was unable to cope with the situation by herself, chose to seek guidance from trusted staff members. One staff member was incredulous to discover the way in which Tracey was managing this conflict situation, after discussions with other equally surprised year level advisors and members of the school administration:

> When I found out by another Year Advisor yesterday . . . I couldn't believe the main reason she was staying away. Tracey's frightened, Tracey's really scared and she won't come to school if this girl's at school – that's how bad it's got. Because she knows if she retaliates, with her track record she's going to be suspended for four days or five days, and she can't afford that to happen. So, rather than that she's just avoiding the whole situation, and would rather stay at home until it is resolved here, so she can come back safely. Which is not Tracey. Definitely not Tracey. Before, she would get a posse and a band behind her and she'd go and confront this girl no matter what creed or colour she is . . . And so the maturity and the coping mechanisms are changing.

This teacher's comments demonstrate Tracey's increasing ability to employ successfully positive approaches to conflict management as opposed to universally negative methods. Her past reliance on aggression has made way for more effective techniques such as 'cooling off' periods and mediation. From this experience, Tracey now recognises the benefits of approaching others for guidance rather than internalising her anxieties and trying to cope with them on her own: 'I never, never approached anyone, just done everything independently'.

This new approach to conflict management has also opened the lines of communication between Tracey and her mother – who was kept informed about Tracey's progress from the Principal and through written correspondence. Now Tracey will 'always talk to Mum, me and Mum are really close. Like, we never used to be, we used to fight all the time and I used to lie to her but now . . .'. Eva confirms that Tracey's approach to conflict management translated from school to home:

Eva: *She'll come to me and talk to me about a conflict that she's having at school and we sort it out together. Or conflict with her brother and sister, and we'll sort that out . . . Yeah, she has changed . . . I've seen a big change in Tracey's behaviour . . . She's just turned around so much . . . we communicate a lot better. We get on, we can talk about anything . . . She'll think before she has her outburst. And then if she's got something to be said she'll say it, but once before with Tracey it would just be stomping, slamming, screaming . . . And now she'll think and everything's . . . we can talk. It's just so pleasant.*

Interviewer: *Is that since the project?*

Eva: *I'd say it is, yes, because everything about Tracey, it just changed. She's completely different at school, at home.*

Cooling Conflict permeated all aspects of her life, including improved relationships with family members, friends and teachers. This in turn had positive side effects, which Tracey herself notes: 'I've improved out of sight. More confident, my attitude, just my attitude towards schoolwork, towards my family, towards the teachers, everything's just changed. It's great'. Changes to Tracey's school and home life tended to appear gradually, which meant that adequate time to reflect was essential in order to ensure that she was able to fully evaluate her experiences.

Tracey's increase in confidence and self-esteem were manifested during the program itself in her leadership role in teaching a large group of primary school students. And like many others, she was able to surprise her teacher with her ability to teach instinctively when the need arose:

A number of people talked about Tracey and I think it opened a lot of people's eyes about the sort of person that Tracey was – people remarking that they were prepared to show initiative and be responsible. And show leadership skills. Tracey's ability to do that really did surprise people.

The program also enabled Tracey to transcend the limitations she placed on herself as well as her everyday anxieties:

Drama takes away your feelings too . . . you forget about a lot of things and you have a lot of fun in there . . . the other day I came in depressed for some reason. And when I was doing my skits and that, I just forgot all about my depression and just let this other character take control inside of me.

Tracey also chose, by enrolling in the subject for Year 9, to sustain the empowering effect of drama, which taught her 'not to be so shamed, [and] not to get embarrassed'. Tracey's mother even attributed to drama the creation of a new person, with a new attitude towards school:

> She's loving her Drama . . . It's doing something for her . . . It's created a different person and she loves it. It's making her want to come to school, it's changed her . . . she's loving every minute of it . . . [Cooling Conflict gave students such as Tracey] a taste of theatre and the power of it and I think they're interested in it. It wasn't just Drama, it was because the social action content of it was relevant to them.

Tracey was able to express her awareness of self-transcendence – the ability to morph into a totally different person until in control of her emotions: 'Now if I am angry I just change into someone else and forget my old self until I am happy again'. These comments offer a remarkable insight into how Tracey copes with her conflict situations, based on what she learnt during the study. By copying appropriately positive behaviour modelled by characters in the various forum theatre pieces she devised, enacted and intervened in, Tracey is able to transfer her learning in the drama classroom directly to the reality of her life and conflict situations.

> Turning your anger into, like, drama, like instead of getting angry and violent, like, you picture yourself doing something else, you know, like, when you're doing it, forum theatre taught you to stop and think before you acted on it.

Without the confidence that drama gave her, Tracey admits that she

> wouldn't have done that, ever, get up in front of the class and be a teacher, anything like that . . . But I have to do something for myself instead of worrying what everyone else has to think and I just like drama, I've never done drama before and when [Cooling Conflict] came to our school, I loved it, I wanted to do it every day . . .

Empathy

The ability to empathise is a key component of drama. Tracey's involvement in both forum theatre and peer teaching assisted her to comprehend conflict situations and the individuals involved in them from a range of perspectives. The leadership she developed here also left her feeling needed, appreciated and useful, and her learning experiences were then able to become much more cooperative, collaborative and reciprocal.

Significantly, the experience of being placed in the role of teacher better enabled Tracey to empathise with her teachers, as she learnt how difficult it is to engage a large group of students over an extended period of time.

I felt sorry for them. I know how they felt when I was mucking up and being loud and I knew how hard it was for them with all the other students. I hate it when someone yells out now . . .

I used to be a loudmouth, back-chatted the teachers, usually if they say something to me I react at them, you know, but now I just stay calm, take a few breaths and just think about things and what kind of trouble it's gonna cause if you just keep biting at 'em and that.

Moreover, for the first time since beginning high school, Tracey's behaviour was no longer considered in need of continual monitoring: 'I had a blue book [a report book for teachers to enter her behaviour every lesson] two whole years straight with only, like a couple of weeks off it. This year I haven't had a blue book at all. Used to have detentions every day'. Her mother confirms this: 'Tracey lived on one of them. Yeah, Tracey lived on a blue book but she's going real well. I haven't seen one actually'.

The recognition and positive reinforcement Tracey subsequently received encouraged her to strive even harder. Two years further on, as Tracey was preparing to begin Year 11, the researchers followed her up again:

Tracey:	*My teachers all tell me that I've improved and they're proud of me all the time.*
Interviewer:	*Such as who?*
Tracey:	*Miss Barr.*
Interviewer:	*Yeah.*
Tracey:	*Mr Morton, Mr Lewis.*
Interviewer:	*Your Mum told you?*
Tracey:	*Yeah, Mum tells me.*
Interviewer:	*And how does that make you feel?*
Tracey:	*Happy and want to keep going and to . . . what's the word, better myself . . . Yeah, love school now. Better than I used to. Hated coming to school, now I love it. I don't, like, pretend I'm sick or anything like that any more. [I used to do that] 'cause it was boring. [But now] I just like coming to school, socialising, getting my work done. I've been getting heaps of awards for good behaviour . . . so I got a scrap book and paste them all in there because there was that many . . . They're for every subject . . . cooperation, participation . . . improvement, outstanding achievement in English . . . I get Drama ones all the time, every day there is Drama. I just look at them and think, 'Oh, how do I get these?' And when I was bad I never, ever got one. Never! And this year I've just got nearly a whole scrapbook full of them.*

Tracey's mother claimed that she was keeping them as a reminder to maintain this standard. This was because Tracey had begun looking ahead to the future.

> *She's got a book at home that she's keeping up now and pasting in for her adult life I'd say . . . she wants to be a policewoman too so for her to continue good behaviour, that's another step for her. She needs to understand that to get into the police force too you need to have no blemishes or stains so she needs . . . she's understanding that too now, how to solve issues rather than fighting.*

We spoke to the school Principal: 'She's fine and going on pretty well. Staying fairly serious and she's got a good attitude. She's been no problem at all . . . She's really turned herself around.' Tracey's teachers acknowledged their hope that such external means of recognition would further encourage her to succeed in other subject areas, and so far, this appeared to be the case, because school was now actually a pleasant experience for Tracey. When Tracey had arguments with peers and friends, she now attempted to 'be open with them and tell them how and what I feel and how can we deal with it'. This new attitude was further reflected in the comments of one of her classmates who was also involved in the program: 'Tracey, a friend of mine, she usually gets into a lot of fights' but ever since the program 'she's backing out and not wanting to fight any more'.

Tracey's success at school permeated her home life. Both mother and daughter have acknowledged their ability to communicate more effectively together. Her mother pointed out that there 'used to be . . . a lot of outbursts and then we'd just yell and scream at one another. Now, Tracey will come home and tell me what's wrong and we'll sit down together and we'll try and work things out more'.

A final word from Tracey . . .

Cooling Conflict facilitated within Tracey a transformation so profound that it completely altered her status as a troublemaker in the school. This negative persona was transcended by the emergence of a girl better equipped to handle not only her conflict situations, but also her relationships with others. In fact these positive outcomes permeated all aspects of her life – school life, social life, home life. This result has been continuously acknowledged by staff, students and Tracey's mother, and by Tracey herself. The program has taught her that she is capable of being a leader, and her story has shown that she is putting this lesson into practice in a myriad of ways, even daring to envisage herself in the career role of policewoman. Tracey is a much happier person with significantly higher levels of confidence and self-esteem. She and others attribute her new sense of competence, learning and empowerment at least partly to the effect that *Cooling Conflict* had on her:

> *It's great . . . It has made me feel like I have got to listen to others and that there are other ways to deal with conflict . . . Ever since I've been doing* Cooling Conflict, *I haven't been getting into trouble at school lately. My results have been really good and so I think it must have done something. My pleasure and thank you for helping.*

. . . And her mother

> *If [Cooling Conflict] can help children, I think it's a must. If that can bring some children out and let them feel what they do feel and express themselves and be taught then how to deal with other issues, it can only better a child. I think it's excellent. From my child's point of view it's been wonderful and she's found a new interest too in Drama, and it's helping her, and I'm proud of the program and I'm proud of her.*

Notes

1. Cockett, S. (1998) What's Real in Drama? *NADIE Journal – Journal of Drama Australia*, vol. 22, no. 2, p. 42.

implementing
the program

introduction

As Part One of the book has explained, *Cooling Conflict* is an approach towards empowering students to manage their conflicts and deal with bullying themselves, and so become leaders in conflict management in their schools and in their communities. The program, when introduced to a school or cluster of schools, particularly with a parallel program of professional development for the teachers, is a highly motivating and exciting approach to whole-school conflict management. It strengthens communication among the different age and cultural groups in the high school, the feeder primary schools and the community, and reinforces the school's collective identity.

The first three chapters have described in detail how the program encourages a whole-school approach to conflict management, and is embedded within the school curriculum. Part One explained how young people learn about how conflict happens and its dynamics, and about the power and abuse of power that result in bullying. Armed with this knowledge, students begin to take control of their own conflicts. The program then sets up the peer teaching structures whereby students not only reinforce their learning, but also begin to generate their own networks of care and support throughout the school. Part One also explained how *Cooling Conflict* uniquely combines two key approaches – educational drama techniques and peer teaching – in a carefully structured sequence.

Part Two now describes step by step how the program is implemented in schools and how it operates in the individual classroom:

○ It starts by teaching a senior class, the **key class**, about the roots and causes of conflict and bullying, and how to practise conflict management through de-escalation and mediation, using carefully structured drama techniques.
○ This class then reinforces their own learning and starts the cycle of empowerment by

teaching the concepts, again through drama, to younger classes in another curricular area, the **first relay classes**. These classes then reinforce their own understanding and are empowered to use the techniques to teach a third group of classes of younger students, either in the school or in local primary schools, the **second relay classes**.

○ These students then take the process further within their own school, sharing their new-found knowledge and power with other relay classes of younger students. In addition, the key and first relay classes may take the process a major step further, into the community, by identifying a significant conflict or issue of bullying and misuse of power that is of local community concern, and devising an interactive theatrical presentation (community theatre in education) to clarify the issues and stimulate healing discussions with the concerned community groups.

○ The parents and the wider community are involved throughout the program's implementation within the school.

The normal implementation of the program begins with a senior drama class in a secondary school and then spreads down through the school via peer teaching. Students from the secondary school then implement *Cooling Conflict* in their neighbouring primary schools, and the primary students they peer teach become peer teachers in turn for younger students in their schools. However, it is also possible for primary schools to implement the program separately within their individual school. In this case, the primary school simply follows exactly the same steps as any secondary school. The only difference is that the all the peer teaching happens within the primary school. Furthermore, students from a primary school where *Cooling Conflict* is operating may want to share their expertise with other primary schools by peer teaching in those schools.

The program's infrastructure

Preparing the school for *Cooling Conflict*

CHAPTER 4

The school infrastructure

Implementing *Cooling Conflict* will place some demands on the school administration, the staff as a whole and the administrative flexibility of the school community. The program has been trialled in schools with very diverse administrative structures and it is designed to fit naturally and with only a small amount of disruption into:

○ the curriculum
○ the school's management and logistical structures
○ the school's social learning agenda.

There are a number of essential elements that must be provided for the program to be successful. The two most important pre-requisites are in the background and hard to quantify but they are crucial to the program's overall success:

○ The school administration is genuinely committed to supporting the program.
○ There is whole-school support for the program's aims. This includes teachers – those not in the program directly, as well as those whose students are engaged in it – the student body, the key support staff like Guidance Officers, Aboriginal Liaison Officers etc., the parents, and the local community leaders.

As usual, this comes down to communication, and *somebody*'s willingness to take the responsibility to create this infrastructure of readiness in the school and community. The research project's most spectacular successes were achieved in schools where that trouble was taken, and the children were supported and affirmed in their developing understanding, with resulting visible change in their behaviour and the school culture. The biggest disappointments were those schools where the program was announced in a blaze of enthusiasm – and frequently good publicity opportunities – and then neglected or taken for granted, so that the students' excitement and sense of enhanced self-worth and social achievement were frittered away, and the program petered out in lack of leadership and logistical problems. If a school is considering adopting *Cooling Conflict*, the most valuable first step is to identify a group of keen people with a stake in improving conflict management and anti-bullying in the school, get them on-side, and start to raise the consciousness of the teachers, parents and administration about this issue, to let them know that this most intractable of school problems can be at least ameliorated, perhaps revolutionised.

And for that, the school first of all has to acknowledge openly that it does have problems with bullying, and its students do have problems with conflict management. This takes courage. A few schools have resisted the invitation to join the program on the grounds that they do not have any bullying or conflict – because they don't see much evidence of it. Some are uneasy, because they believe that to admit a bullying problem or endemic conflict will stigmatise the school – and perhaps risk valuable fees or enrolments. That's where the courage lies. Conflict and bullying exist in all schools, because large numbers of culturally and temperamentally diverse people, at different maturation levels and with many competing and even incompatible interests, are lumped together in structures where the balance of power is very complex and many-layered, and an explicit or implicit component of nearly every decision made. Those schools that proclaim loudest their freedom from bullying and conflict problems are often those where evidence of these very problems strikes the outsider as soon as you walk through the gate.

Establishing a management structure

Following these pre-requisites of ambience and school culture, there are some more down-to-earth pre-requisites in order for the program to work successfully:

There is a senior teacher/administrator willing to act as Cooling Conflicts *coordinator, preferably at deputy head level*

Especially in the secondary school, the difficulties of matching timetables, teacher release if there is an in-service program, even minor curriculum modification and general intra-mural communication all demand that somebody with a power and influence in the school is in charge, committed to the program.

There is a trained or experienced drama teacher, the key class teacher

Although the drama teaching works down through the schools without necessarily any drama-trained involvement (when the relay classes prepare for and teach their peers), we have found it valuable to have one person on-site with that expertise, to lead the key class. It is valuable for the first class entrusted with the task of conveying the knowledge to another to have every opportunity to master the drama skills that both convey and demonstrate the knowledge. For another thing, a teacher who is passionate about drama is invariably keen to raise the status of the subject in the school, and to contribute to the general pastoral and curricular health. For a third, many non-drama-trained teachers (and sometimes students) are either entirely unaware of drama's pedagogical possibilities, or nervous about their ability to utilise them.

There is a suitable key class

This is normally a senior high school drama class, who are (or should be) committed to exploring conflict through drama, used to stepping into others' shoes, who are familiar with working in drama, work well together, and are mature in terms of the school community. If you are thinking of starting the program at middle school or even upper primary level, because there is no local high school or high school able or willing to begin the program, you may well have a class of younger students with all these characteristics.

There are appropriate younger relay classes (not drama) available and with willing teachers

These may be found by looking at the curriculum – as we have already seen in Chapters 1 and 2, doing *Cooling Conflict* is a way of teaching plenty of curricular topics in many subject areas. On the other hand choosing the first relay classes may need to be subject to the lottery of the timetable. The most difficult logistical element of the whole program is matching the classes' availability for peer teaching. In some secondary schools (but by no means all), the inflexible complexity of the timetable will necessitate special arrangements being made for these pivotal sessions. Other occasional ambushes lurk, like exams and field trips, to disrupt the flow of the peer teaching.

The primary school(s) and teachers to be involved are interested and willing

This is in our experience the least problematic of these demands – it is often easier for primary schools to flex their timetables, and there is less at stake in acknowledging that young children have problems with bullying and conflict. However, if the program is beginning in a high school and spreading to local primary schools, these schools must be part of the planning and consultation process from the beginning.

A school management committee is established

The school **management committee** must be committed to ensure the effective working of *Cooling Conflicts* throughout the school and be prepared to deal with problems that may arise. In the case of a high school, this will probably include:

○ the Principal (who may not be involved in the day-to-day management)
○ the *Cooling Conflicts* coordinator
○ the key class teacher
○ one first relay class teacher
○ one relay class teacher from each contributing primary school
○ and at least one student (from the key class in the first instance).

This committee should convene at the outset of the program to develop the planning process and the timeline. The committee should then meet as necessary – if the program is running well, this need not be often. However, it should meet at the end of each year's cycle to evaluate the program and make whatever modifications are necessary in advance for next year.

Sequence and timeline

Cooling Conflict is designed to operate in an ongoing sequence of annual cycles, each with at least two and up to four phases. In a full version of the program, it will roll down the age range from the senior secondary to the lower primary – in a standard binary school system, a high school with one or more of its feeder primary schools. As already noted, it can also be started in a middle school, or even the top of a primary school.

This *Cooling Conflict* timetable is the model that we have found to work best in most situations. However, each school context is different, and many variations are possible.

Preparation (the previous year and term one)

Classes and teachers are chosen, in-service carried out (see below), and peer-teaching timelines organised.

Phase 1 (term 1 or 2, six weeks to one term)

A **key class** (e.g. Year 11 Drama) learns about the structures and nature of conflict and bullying through a range of drama techniques, including enhanced forum theatre (EFT). They are split into groups, each to meet a class of younger children, their **first relay class** (e.g. Year 9 English). The key class finds out about those students' conflict and bullying problems and devise a program of EFT to teach the conflict/bullying concepts that they have learned to the younger students. Each group spends up to five lessons teaching the relay class (as part of the relay class's English studies) through EFT and other drama activities, during which the younger students learn the conflict and bullying concepts, and also how to create their own EFT.

Phase 2 (term 2 or 3, three to four weeks)

The **relay class** and their teacher then devise a program of EFT to teach what they have learned to another group of still younger students, the **second relay class** (e.g. Year 7, as part of Studies of Society).

Phase 3 (term 3, three to four weeks)

In their turn, the **second relay class** and their teacher devise a program of EFT to teach what they have learned to another group of still younger students, the **third relay class** (e.g. Year 5, as part of Health and Personal Development studies).

Phase 4 (term 4, three weeks)

In their turn, the **third relay class** and their teacher devise a program of EFT to teach what they have learned to another group of still younger students, the fourth relay class (e.g. Year 3, as part of Studies of Society again).

Additional phase (term 3 or 4)

Almost certainly, having completed their peer teaching the key and upper relay classes will be feeling very confident in what they know about conflict and bullying, and disappointed that the program has come to an end for them. If the school's curriculum is sufficiently flexible, now is the time to give any of those classes the opportunity to spread their new-found wisdom within the wider community of the school or neighbourhood, and also spread their wings dramatically, by creating a piece of community theatre in education (see Chapter 7) to address a particular school or community problem, that may be showcased in or outside the school.

In the following years, new classes of students should be given the opportunity to take part in the program. It may be possible and productive, in some cases, for one of last year's first relay classes to be next year's key class.

Identifying the program classes

The program builds on young people's own natural desire to gain control and mastery over the conflicts in their lives. They will get a lot of new understanding and life skills, without going outside their normal curriculum. The major advantages are in self-esteem and social development. The relay classes appreciate, as a real privilege, being taught by their peers. The key and older relay classes gain pride, confidence and satisfaction from the peer teaching. All enjoy the drama work and can recognise the value of developing their conflict handling skills and understanding.

The key classes

In the secondary school the key class or classes should preferably be Year 10 or 11 Drama students with some experience. In primary schools the key classes chosen would normally be the most senior in the school. It is valuable for key class students to have the drama skills to manage and model the initial peer teaching, and the maturity and confidence to grasp the key concepts and lead the program. However, they will need to spend a considerable period of time on the program – ideally the majority of a term's work – so it needs to be carefully integrated into the class's curriculum work, perhaps by providing a full unit of study. Assessment can be built into it as a natural part of the learning program for that class.

The first relay classes

The first relay classes should be younger students (in a high school, Years 7, 8 or 9). The ideal age gap between themselves and the key class is two years. The number of first relay classes will be dictated by the number of key class students, who will be peer teaching the relay classes in groups of between four and eight. These group sizes are important. There must be enough key class students to give each other confidence during the peer teaching, and spread the load of taking a whole class for complex drama tasks, like running preparatory activities, organising groupwork, and leading group discussions. On the other hand, too many key class students in the one relay class will create confusion and unfocused activities. Therefore if the key class has 24 students, there could be between three and six first relay classes.

The relay classes can be drawn from a number of subject areas. They should *not* be drama classes or else the program may be seen to be the province only of Drama, not the whole school. As with the key class, the specific curricular area is crucial, since for them too the program is part of their normal work. They will probably not spend so long on the program – all told, including the time they are themselves being peer-taught, perhaps ten or twelve classes over four or five weeks.

Later relay classes

Carrying through the third and fourth phases of the program with new, younger peer students is very important. In the first place, the peer teaching is, for *all* the students, by far the most significant, empowering and exciting part of the program – by peer teaching, the relay classes reinforce their own understanding just as the key classes have. Furthermore, by teaching the program, the relay class students become leaders in conflict management and mentors for the younger students they teach, either within the school or with primary students who will be moving to the high school within a year.

Primary students in a large number of schools involved in the program have proved fully capable of grasping the key concepts about conflict and bullying, particularly when made concrete and comprehensible through the drama. They have also proved to be competent peer teachers at least down to Year 3, and Year 1 students have responded enthusiastically to being taught by their peers. However, the peer teaching that the very young students receive from their peer teachers will probably not be so long or sustained, and the drama techniques may be simplified. The teacher needs to choose the curricular area (or integrated area) whose time the program will occupy. The logistics of the peer teaching for the primary teacher may be easier – timetable lines and inflexible syllabuses are usually less of an issue in primary schools.

Space

This program does not make high demands on space, but there are some requirements. For the key class work, whatever space is normally used for drama will be quite adequate. For the relay classes, it is usually preferable for the peer teaching to take place in their normal classrooms if possible – with the drama strategies tailored to fit – provided that some open space can be cleared within the classrooms. The relay class students are 'at home' and likely to take the program work more in their stride if they are in a familiar space. If however, the occasion is a 'special occasion' such as a primary school induction day, it would be helpful if the peer teachers can be given a larger than normal space to work in.

In-service and professional development

It should be possible to implement *Cooling Conflict* entirely by following this book. The basic drama methods, and the peer teaching structures, have been designed for teachers with no prior experience of either. However, effective scaffolding by the school is essential if the teachers involved are to achieve the best results from the program. To begin with, a broadly based **in-service** is needed to raise the awareness of the whole staff and give them a sense of ownership of the program. This in turn will help the teachers to support the students appropriately as they develop their own new knowledge, enabling them to assist individual students in their own life conflict and power battles, and to provide the support networks that will be the real mark of success for the school as a whole.

The implementation of *Cooling Conflict* in a school should therefore begin with a three-step in-service program. The **in-service** program needs to be led by the *Cooling Conflict* **coordinator** and the **key teacher**, with the involvement of a drama advisory service if one is available, or drama educators at the local university. Outside advisors and educators will need to read this chapter and Chapter 6 first, so they know exactly what they are supposed to do! Most experienced drama educators now are familiar with the basic forum theatre technique, and they ought also to understand the process drama techniques used to enhance it in the program. Their involvement may help to provide status to the whole program.

Step 1: introducing *Cooling Conflict*

Book 20–30 minutes at a full staff meeting to introduce the program and go over the basic principles – give the staff a brief glimpse of the vision and how you are going to go about it, and invite their help.

Step 2: training the *Cooling Conflict* staff

This is done most effectively by a whole day in-service program that brings together the **relay teachers** in the school and at least one relay teacher from each participating primary school. This would be a good time to ask the drama advisor to come in and lead part of the day.

The best time for this is not at the very start of the program, but after the key class has been working at the program, and is developing their own drama for their peers, but before they actually hit the first relay classes. The day should consist of the following:

○ An introduction, comprising

 –a general introduction to the principles of the program

 –a summary of how it will work, with the timeline.

 (You will find helpful handouts or overheads in Appendix 2.)

○ A practical workshop, taking the teachers experientially through the actual process of creating a piece of enhanced forum theatre (use the method described in Chapter 6). Once teachers experience the actual drama techniques at the heart of the program they invariably have a clear understanding of their function and confidence in their effectiveness. This session should finish with a reflective discussion, where the key teacher and any drama advisor can deal with the issues that have arisen.

○ If the key class is actively involved at the time of the in-service, some of them might be invited in to give a brief demonstration – a dummy run for their own forthcoming appointment with pedagogy – or to share a little of their experience in discussion with the teachers.

○ A final logistics session, sorting out how and when the various peer teaching encounters will take place – particularly those where a visit across schools is involved.

Step 3: hands-on help

It is also valuable for the key teacher or an external advisor to be made available to come into the classroom of any relay teacher who is still feeling insecure, and help them with their planning and implementation of the next stage of the drama work, following the visit of their own peer teachers. This is best organised on this model:

○ A joint planning session

○ One lesson taught basically by the visitor, with the class teacher as auxiliary

○ Another lesson taught basically by the class teacher with the visitor as auxiliary

○ A third lesson taught by the class teacher, with the visitor observing and side-coaching (or available for advice afterwards).

Steps 2 and 3 are not without financial implications, however.

Financial costs

The program is not expensive, and some or all of the costs can often be absorbed as 'in-kind' resourcing. However, there are financial implications to implementing *Cooling Conflict*. The first essential cost is a small one – that of providing all the participants in the program with a copy of this book.

The second and major cost is an optional one, choosing to implement either or both of steps 2 and 3 of the in-service program. Step 2 will entail release and a day's teacher relief for all the participants, and perhaps a fee for the outside expert if you are using one. Step 3 will entail a fee for the outside advisor, or teacher relief costs for the key teacher.

The third cost is dependent on the context: travel expenses for that phase in the program where the students of one school visit the other – and possibly for accompanying teacher release. If you are implementing *Cooling Conflict* in an all-age school, or a campus where primary and secondary are together or close by, this may not be an issue.

A small expense that will be well worthwhile, but is again optional, is that involved in formally documenting and evaluating the program on an ongoing basis. That might include getting questionnaires (see Appendix 2) printed and the results collated, or hiring a research assistant to conduct student interviews.

Documentation and evaluation

There are a number of ways to keep track of how well the program is operating. First, there are some actual measures you can take – by instituting a record of the reported incidences and types of bullying in the school, and seeing over time whether there are any changes to this, as *Cooling Conflict* becomes established in the school. However, this kind of quantitative data can be very misleading, and needs careful interpretation – an increase in the incidence of reporting bullying might indicate that there is more of it, or conversely that students are just feeling more secure in reporting it. Some kinds of bullying may be more easily or safely reported than others, too. Another measure would be to look at changed behaviour in school and classroom. Most schools have some form of sanctions to control or reduce bad behaviour in habitual misbehavers. Monitoring this within the classes directly involved in *Cooling Conflict* can provide useful and occasionally startling data – as in the case of Tracey, described in Chapter 3.

Questionnaires to the students are useful, too – and these actually form part of the program (see Appendix 2). The most useful questionnaires, of course, are those administered after the program.

In many ways, however, qualitative data can be more helpful than the figures, especially taken in tandem with them. For key and relay class teachers to keep notes and interview some students alone and in focus groups, or even do their own small-scale case studies, is very revealing. The program coordinator will need to be aware of the activity that is going on, and make an effort to collate it so that it can be used each year to inform the ongoing program planning.

Outcomes for the whole-school community

Through the implementation of *Cooling Conflict*, a range of classes across both secondary and primary schools will learn about conflict and bullying management using drama techniques. The students must then be supported to become the vanguard in building a culture that minimises bullying and provides escapes for all parties, and sustains a healthy conflict management and cultural relations agenda in the school. This is where the whole-school commitment to examine and deal with conflict and bullying, and to face the racism and antagonisms that may exist in the school, becomes of paramount importance.

Through peer teaching, the students learn from each other, and in turn are empowered to teach their fellow students. The strongest learning lies here with the peer teachers, as they reinforce their own learning of the key concepts of conflict management and intercultural relationships in the process, in order to teach it to their peers. If what they learn is affirmed and given reinforcement by the teachers and administration, it will spread through the school. The first result is that the older class automatically becomes the younger class's mentors – they have the shared affective experience, and they have the required distance from each other to provide confidence. The younger students develop the confidence that their problems are understood by somebody at their own level, but more powerful than they are. For the older students their self-esteem comes with knowing they are responsible for vulnerable people they have already helped, some slightly, some significantly.

This does not happen overnight, or even over-year. If the program is sustained over a period, and allowed to grow, then eventually a large proportion, most or even all of the school students can have had the opportunity to experience the program at one level or more – last year's first relay class may become next year's key class, and students fresh from primary school emerge when the program commences for the year in a high school, talking knowledgeably of latent, emerging and manifest conflict.

If the **community theatre in education** is implemented, students even become theatrical ambassadors in bullying and conflict management for the school's neighbourhood community.

In other words this program is explicitly aimed at having an effect on the whole school. It will already be evident that the dissemination of the concepts and ethos of the program throughout the school, directly or indirectly, is of paramount importance. The program lends itself to a high profile, to creating a 'buzz' round the school, at student and staff level – and in the local community. Some of the students will feel important and empowered and behaviour changes may be evident. This should be encouraged and the key and relay class students given publicity for their participation.

The staff too are important – and not just those directly participating in the program. All the staff should be encouraged to feel ownership of the program and should be able to involve themselves: by observation and reporting, by advice, and by facilitating the possible logistical difficulties of timetabling. Perhaps the single most effective strategy here is to involve other teachers and welfare personnel, not just the key and relay class teachers, and if there is any kind of preliminary in-service (see above), encourage some of them to attend.

Other ways in which the whole school can be kept in touch with the program include relay class teachers taking the program further. Following Phases 1 and 2, relay class teachers who are inspired by the peer teaching or the work of their own classes might swap classes with colleagues who have not been exposed to the program.

Involving the parents

Although this appears last in the description of the implementation of the program in the school, it should begin when the program begins, and is crucial to its success. First of all, the vast majority of parents are deeply concerned with the problems of conflict and bullying in schools, and are only too willing to support any initiative. This home support is invaluable in scaffolding the concepts and behaviour. Secondly, the research has shown that support for the program from individual parents has been crucial in the transformation in behaviour that has occurred in some difficult and aggressive students. Thirdly, the approval of parents not only gives the program, and the school, a higher status, but also becomes part of the culture change the program aims to achieve.

Parents can be informed about the program at the very beginning through letters home that explain about *Cooling Conflict* and seek their approval for their children to be involved. A regular section in the school newsletter or a separate *Cooling Conflict* newsletter can then provide regular updates. More actively, students can also be encouraged to take home information about the program, and to seek their parents' assistance in learning more about conflict and bullying.

It is also important to bring parents into the program.

○ This can be done by holding information sessions at the beginning and during the course of *Cooling Conflict,* by having open sessions of the program at certain times so parents can actually see their children at work on it.

○ Parents can also be invited to attend performances of the **enhanced forum theatre** plays created by the students after they have performed them as part of their peer teaching.

○ Finally, if a **theatre in education** play is developed as the additional phase of the program, this is an opportunity to involve parents in all aspects of the performance – sets, costume, lighting and of course transport.

The program's structure

Teaching the program in the classroom

Cooling Conflict is designed to operate as a whole-school program that engages all students in the school, both as learners and as teachers. Chapter 4 outlined how this is achieved through the use of peer teaching, with senior key classes teaching younger relay classes. These students then become peer teachers themselves to even younger students in their school, who in turn teach even younger relay classes.

Chapter 5 describes in depth how the levels of peer teaching operate, providing an overview for the peer teaching and the classroom activities required to make it work effectively, and detailing the learning experiences and outcomes of the program.

The key class

It is the senior students in a school who initiate the whole *Cooling Conflict* program, and are the key to the success of the program. For this reason these senior students are known as the **key class**. Ideally, the involvement of the senior drama students should continue for the whole school year, but this is often not possible. Their key contribution is actually made in just one term of 10 weeks, and the program for key classes works most successfully as a whole-term project, taught within a relevant curriculum unit.

In a secondary school the key class would normally be a Year 11 or Year 10 Drama class, and the relevant unit could be Improvisation, Political theatre or Playbuilding. The program then becomes a part of the normal drama curriculum and is taught and assessed just like any other unit. Similarly, if *Cooling Conflict* is being introduced at the senior level of a primary school, the key class unit of study could be in Health and Physical Education, English, Studies of Society or indeed Drama. In this way the students acquire valuable and relevant skills and knowledge that will flow through into the rest of their studies.

In the second year of the *Cooling Conflict* program in a school, these key class students may still be involved in the program as peer teachers once more. However, if they are in Year 12 this would be difficult, and if they were the senior class in a primary school, they will have moved on. The research has demonstrated that where the key class peer teachers from one year remain in the school the following year, they tend to become mentors and positive role models for the younger students, even if they are no longer actively involved in *Cooling Conflict*.

The first relay classes

These students are so-called, because they are the first to whom the torch of knowledge is relayed by their peer teachers, and in turn they pass on the precious baton to younger students. In secondary schools the first relay classes are Years 7–9, depending on the year level of the key class and practical constraints such as timetabling. As we indicated in the previous chapter, the program works best with a two or three year gap between each level of peer teaching.

The program can be initiated in any subject in the curriculum where a unit on conflict is appropriate. The relay classes chosen should *not* be Drama classes, or at the least not exclusively. *Cooling Conflict* is a whole-school program and should not be seen as the preserve of drama. Rather, its value should be seen to be applicable across the entire curriculum, so that it is embedded in the students' learning. The research has shown that the *Cooling Conflict* program fits into many areas of the curriculum in Years 7–9 in secondary schools, as indicated above for the key class.

If *Cooling Conflict* is to be implemented directly into a primary school, the first relay classes would normally be found in Years 3–5, again depending on the year level of the key class and the organisation within the school. Once more the program should be initiated as part of the normal school curriculum, and should be seen as relevant, and indeed essential, to learning in the school.

In the next year of *Cooling Conflict* in a school, if they remain as a discrete class these first relay students would normally become key class peer teachers, helping to continue the dissemination of the program throughout the school. This occurs both formally through the peer teaching, and – just as important – informally as these students become mentors and role models for the younger ones. Where the program has begun in a secondary school, the first relay class students can mentor those students coming from primary schools who have already been involved in peer teaching. This is particularly important as worldwide research on bullying indicates that the bullying of Year 7 and 8 students by Year 10 students is the most common form of bullying in secondary schools. Through *Cooling Conflict*, older secondary students get to know the younger students when they teach them in their primary schools, and then teach them again in their first year of high school.

The second relay classes

The second relay classes will normally be primary school students, whether the program begins in a secondary or a primary school.

If the first relay peer teachers are from a high school, then the second relay classes will be chosen from Years 5–7, depending on the needs and availabilities of the classes and the logistics of the peer teaching. In this case the second relay classes will go on to peer teach younger students in their school, Years 1–4, so that these younger classes become the third wave of relay students.

If the program has commenced in a primary school, the second relay classes will be chosen from the junior primary levels, Years 1–3.

The youngest relay class students will become peer teachers in the *Cooling Conflict* program as they progress through the school and into secondary school. As with the key and first and second relay classes, these relay students become leaders in the school and mentors and role models for the younger students as they progress. Gradually therefore, the culture of the school and the yard changes, with networks of support replacing or at least alleviating the cliques of 'difference' and 'status'.

The phases of the program

The *Cooling Conflict* program operates in four phases. The first three of these involve peer teaching about bullying and conflict using drama in classrooms ranging from Year 11 to Year 1. The fourth phase is optional and involves taking the program into the community through a theatre in education performance.

The peer teaching of the fundamental bullying and conflict concepts, and the use of enhanced forum theatre, remain the same in all the three classroom stages, but these are taught at the level appropriate to the ages of the target classes.

The timing of the phases outlined below will of course depend on the individual schools and classes involved in the program.

The peer teaching component is the most motivating part of the program. The more peer teaching that occurs, the greater the learning, especially for the peer teachers.

Phase one (four weeks)

The nature of conflict and the use of drama

This is the foundation stone of the whole program, with a dual emphasis on giving the key class both a solid understanding of the structures of conflict and bullying and how they are managed, and the basic skills in the use of enhanced forum theatre.

It is essential that the key class students become completely confident in understanding and identifying the conflict and bullying stages of **latent**, **emerging** and **manifest** explained in Chapter 1 and in using the terminology accurately. This is achieved by using a range of improvised dramas suggested by the teacher and students. These scenarios can be completely fictional or based on examples retold by members of the class from their own experiences.

The main drama strategy used in weeks 1–4 is **enhanced forum theatre**, although the students may also use other kinds of role-play, **process drama** and improvised dramatic action to flesh out their understanding of the nature of conflict. Drama teachers should feel free to use whatever other forms of improvised drama they feel confident with. **Enhanced forum theatre** is explained in detail in Chapter 6.

Phase two (six weeks)

Meeting the first relay classes (one lesson)

By arrangement with the teachers, sub-groups from the key class (see 'Logistics' on page 90) visit their chosen first relay class and introduce themselves. At this stage they give the relay students a brief outline of the *Cooling Conflict* program and their part in it, and administer the conflict management questionnaire (Appendix 2). We strongly recommend that the key class groups meet the younger classes they will work with before the peer teaching begins. This gives them a familiarity with the students they will teach and builds anticipation in the younger classes. The questionnaire provides the key class groups with the information about the conflicts and bullying their relay classes typically face and their understanding of conflict. It also gives them a straightforward and unthreatening task to help them break the ice. Using the data from the questionnaires, the teacher and key class students can decide on the conflicts to be explored and the dramatic form to be used.

Developing the peer teaching (2–3 weeks)

Having met their relay classes, the key groups now prepare to instruct them, assisted by the teacher, particularly with effective teaching strategies and classroom management techniques, both for the drama and the conflict and bullying concepts.

○ Each group decides its strategies firstly for teaching the stages of conflict and bullying, either through team teaching or giving particular responsibilities to individuals.

○ The group then decides on appropriate drama games and activities to warm up their classes, allocating responsibility for leading these activities within the group.

○ Finally, the key groups prepare the enhanced forum theatre that they will model to the relay class, devising the drama and rehearsing it until they are competent.

In the last session or two, it is valuable for the key class sub-groups each to try out their opening games and part of their forum theatre with the rest of the class in a 'dummy run'.

Key group peer teaching (3–4 weeks)

The key class sub-groups teach their relay classes. This might take place for every lesson of the fortnight, but in the first week in particular it is vital for the key groups to have time to replan and reflect. If all their lessons run at the same time as the relay classes, it would be preferable for the key groups to teach one lesson, then have the next lesson time to meet and reflect. If timetable constraints prevent this, it is possible for the entire teaching to take place intensively in a single day.

○ The peer teaching encounters will probably start with warm-up games, to break the ice and overcome the nerves and shyness of both classes.

○ The key groups next teach their classes the stages of conflict or bullying, and the basic underlying theory that they have learned, using enhanced forum theatre.

○ The key groups break the relay class into smaller sub-groups, each facilitated by a key class student, to develop their own enhanced forum theatre plays, in order to share and explore conflict or bullying and their management.

○ Each of these is then usually shared with the other sub-groups as interactive audience.

Phase three (a minimum 4 weeks, or until the school runs out of relay classes)

The first relay class prepares (2–3 weeks)

The first relay class students work in sub-groups to prepare their peer teaching. During this time the first relay class students should visit their second relay classes if possible and administer the questionnaire (Appendix 2).

Having learned about bullying and conflict management through the use of enhanced forum theatre and learned its skills from their peer teachers, the first relay class now prepares for their peer teaching in exactly the same way as the key class did in Phase One. Their teachers assist the classes with their planning and particularly with the actual teaching and classroom strategies they will use.

If the time can be spared and the timetable permits, the key class has a potential further role to play in Phase Three in assisting the relay class in its preparation for teaching their second relay classes. The first relay class may for instance need further peer teaching to make the students really competent in the drama techniques.

First relay peer teaching (3–4 weeks)

The first relay sub-groups teach their second relay classes. This can take place as separate lessons in a particular subject spread over the weeks, or may be done intensively in whole mornings and afternoons or even in a single day (if for example, primary school students travel to the local high school for a *Cooling Conflict* day).

Ongoing relays of peer teaching (flexible)

The second relay class students work in exactly the same way as the key and first relay classes did in Phases One to Three, forming into sub-groups to prepare and teach younger students in their schools – the next wave of relay classes. These second relay sub-groups teach the same bullying and conflict concepts as the key and first relay peer teachers did, using the same drama techniques of enhanced forum theatre. However, the peer teaching will obviously be planned to be at the level appropriate to the age of the students being taught. It is here that the classroom teachers can be of most assistance in helping their students to plan their teaching and their classroom management.

Given the flexibility primary schools have in structuring their schedules, this part of the program can be spread over a number of weeks, or may be done intensively within a single week or throughout a number of entire days.

Phase four

Reaching the community

This is an optional phase of the program, which is designed to extend the impact of *Cooling Conflict* into the community, and provide the key and early relay classes with the opportunity to follow up their early contribution to the program with an exciting and useful major project. This fourth phase involves a theatre in education project, conducted towards the end of the school year, or even the following year. In this stage students who have already been peer teachers in the program create a piece of interactive theatre in education about bullying or conflict that is of direct concern to a community audience. This is then performed to that audience (or audiences). Full explanation and steps for implementing this are given in Chapter 7. If it is possible, the key class should be involved in this project, either as organisers, performers or facilitators – or all three.

Learning outcomes in the *Cooling Conflict* program

The outcomes of the *Cooling Conflict* unit are exactly the same for the key and all the relay classes – and for the school as a whole.

By the end of the *Cooling Conflict* program, students should:

○ have developed an understanding of the nature and terminology of bullying and conflict and specifically the three stages – *latent, emerging* and *manifest*
○ have acquired a basic knowledge of simple conflict mediation procedures
○ be able to identify the causes of bullying and conflict and the way they escalate from stage to stage
○ have acquired a clear understanding of specific dramatic activities valuable for teaching conflict management – notably enhanced forum theatre
○ be acquainted with the potential of drama to help them to understand and manage a range of bullying and conflict situations
○ have explored a variety of dramatised bullying and conflict situations, identifying the nature and stage of the dramatised conflicts and experimenting with strategies for managing them
○ have been empowered to successfully manage real bullying and conflict in their own lives, applying the knowledge and strategies acquired in exploring dramatised conflicts
○ have been given the opportunity to enhance their knowledge and skills in bullying and conflict management through peer teaching younger students about conflict

○ have successfully completed a structured learning program designed to enhance harmony in school environments

○ have become active, on-going participants in a self-sustaining whole-school bullying and conflict management program.

Learning experiences

(See also Chapters 6 and 7 for detailed explanation of the drama techniques.)

As the outcomes listed above indicate, the nature of the learning in the *Cooling Conflict* program is the same for all students at all levels. Whilst senior key class students may develop a highly sophisticated understanding of the application of *Cooling Conflict* in their own lives and relationships, junior primary students in the third wave of relay classes have proved capable of articulating, and applying, the principles of bullying and conflict management they have been taught by older students.

The nature and stages of bullying and conflict

The students are introduced to the nature of conflict as a fundamental element in human life and are made familiar with the three stages of both conflict and the kind of conflict known as bullying – **latent**, **emerging** and **manifest** – and the imbalances of **rights**, **interests** and **power** that lead to conflict. In the case of bullying, it always includes an imbalance of power, and the students will learn to identify the different types of bullying – physical, verbal, psychological, social and sexual. Through questioning and the use of metaphors and examples, the students develop a clear understanding of the three stages and how conflict and bullying **escalate**. At this stage the concept is introduced that both conflict and bullying can be managed, **mediated** and **de-escalated** (see Chapter 1 for detailed explanation of these terms).

Using **freeze-frames**, the students work in groups to create three images of a conflict or episode of bullying they have experienced or know about at the three stages of latent, emerging and manifest. It is vital that the students understand that conflicts move through the stages at different times, and the **freeze-frames** will show key moments that may be days, weeks or months apart.

The students discuss a range of conflicts and types of bullying and their causes – both real and fictional – and explore them through the use of freeze-frames and playbuilding techniques such as those described in Chapter 7. They also begin to experiment with attempting to manage the conflicts by manipulating the dramas. For example, the students observing a sequence of three freeze-frames showing the stages of conflict or bullying can step in to alter the gestures and implied interactions in one of the frames in a way that might help to de-escalate the conflict.

Working in groups, the students create sustained improvisations about conflict or bullying containing three scenes depicting the three stages of the conflict. The most immediately effective way of devising these scenes is to improvise a scene of emerging or manifest conflict, then jump back to its causes (its latent phase) and forward again to see the progress and effects of the escalation. Some of these conflicts will be based on real-life stories, some fictional, and they should include cultural issues and difference as an important and relevant cause of both conflict and bullying. These improvisations should also explore the possibilities for managing those dramatised conflicts, both by the participants within the drama, and by observers of the drama stepping in to mediate the conflict or to de-escalate it.

The dramatic form – enhanced forum theatre

This stage begins with the students acquiring an understanding of, and competence in, the use of **enhanced forum theatre** as a form of drama, which allows them to explore conflicts and to experiment with actively managing them. The teacher provides a brief overview of the work of **Augusto Boal**, focusing on the use of **forum theatre** to empower people to change the oppression in their lives.

The students work in groups using enhanced forum theatre to explore a range of conflicts, constructing each play in three scenes, each of which depicts an incident in the three stages of the conflict – the first scene *latent*, the second *emerging*, the third *manifest*. The third scene ends in a crisis or confrontation. These forum plays are performed for the other groups, who are encouraged to **intervene** to take the roles of any of the participants and to de-escalate the conflict.

The students may not immediately grasp the idea that serious conflicts take a long time to germinate and have deep roots, so the scenes they generate sometimes move immediately through the three stages within a few minutes. An important constraint in this period is to impose a minimum time lapse between scenes – say at least a week, a month or even a year.

At this stage the students also fully develop their understanding and use of the **host** as the controller of the drama and learn to identify the use of **magic** by participants. In preparing their pieces, the groups consciously provide opportunities in each scene, at each stage of the conflict, for effective **interventions** to occur.

Although the techniques of **process drama** are more complex than forum theatre, so too can be the resulting understanding about **conflict** and **bullying**. To use process drama is a valuable additional step to give the key class a deeper understanding of conflict and how it operates. If the key class teacher is experienced in the use of these techniques, it is very worthwhile to create some process drama to deepen their understanding of conflict, bullying and their causes. It has not always been found practicable to ask for the key class to devise their own process dramas to peer teach, or for non-drama relay class teachers to master process drama. Accordingly, some of the techniques from process drama have been incorporated within the enhanced forum theatre that is the main peer teaching technique used by the key class.

A particularly important note for the key and first relay teachers

Do not intervene in the peer teaching too quickly or too often . . . if at all! You will be watching the students, and especially at the beginning they will be tentative and the atmosphere uncertain, and the peer teachers will make mistakes. However, left to it, they will certainly take up the challenge and provide effective teaching, even if not exactly how you would do it. Particularly, don't intervene where they are faced with the unexpected – unless it involves physical danger or serious transgression of rules. Let them work their way out of it. The experience will give them enormous satisfaction and the younger classes will respect them more for it. The relay class students don't expect perfect teaching – they do not judge their peers as they do you!

Younger relay class teachers should similarly give their peer teachers the freedom to make mistakes and learn to cope with the demands of teaching. However, as these peer teachers will be primary aged students, sometimes junior primary, some discreet scaffolding and coaching whilst they are teaching will enhance both the teaching and the learning that is occurring.

Assessment

Cooling Conflict provides a range of opportunities for effective and relevant assessment for students.

Process and performance

For senior secondary Drama students, specific outcomes related to student work in devising and performing improvised drama could be assessed at a number of stages in the unit.

When the students are learning to manipulate the styles of forum theatre and process drama in weeks three and four, their abilities to manage the forms and apply them in improvised performance can be assessed, as can their ability to work as part of a cooperative ensemble.

When they are working in their teaching groups to devise their forum plays or process dramas, the process of forming this work can obviously be assessed. When they perform these pieces to the relay classes as models, then performance outcomes can be assessed.

Written reflection

For all students involved in the program at every level, the keeping of a reflective account or journal of their involvement in the *Cooling Conflict* program should be an essential task. These journals are valuable for the students in recording their involvement and encouraging detailed reflection on their learning about bullying and conflict. They are also useful as assessment instruments in measuring the student's achievement of a range of outcomes. For younger students journals are also an essential tool in enhancing literacy.

A very valuable form of written outcome is *writing in-role* where the students are asked to create letters, reports or diary entries, and even poems or 'newspaper interviews', as if they were one of the characters they have been playing or watching – i.e. telling the conflict or bullying story from the character's point of view. From this it is very easy to infer how much understanding of the causes and dynamics of the conflict, and the basic concepts of the program, the students have grasped.

Assignments and tests

Set assignments and tests applied at different stages throughout the unit can be useful in measuring specific outcomes for bullying and conflict management. These can also supply the resources the students need for their work. For Year 11 Drama students, a research assignment on Augusto Boal would obviously increase the students' understanding of forum theatre, just as some further study about process drama would lead to greater competence in using the techniques.

Assessment should begin by acknowledging and evaluating the very considerable effort that is inevitably put into *Cooling Conflict*. An over-enthusiastic or over-meticulous approach to assessment may lead the students to feel that they are being put under unfair pressure, given the considerable personal risks that they are taking. It may even detract from their performance in drama or peer teaching by leading them to be over-cautious or over-dependent on planned procedures. An important part of any peer teaching and of *Cooling Conflict* in particular are the inspired, even radical, changes of plan on instinct or quick negotiation by the students to get themselves out of trouble, and some method of acknowledging and rewarding this within the assessment should be found.

Logistics

Peer teaching ratios

The ratio of peer teachers to peer students is very important. Exactly how the peer teaching is organised will vary in each school, but is likely to involve both whole-class teaching and working with sub-groups of each class. The peer teachers will themselves need to work in sub-groups, both for devising and presenting the work and for teaching their own relay sub-groups. This is for a number of reasons:

○ There need to be enough students in each sub-group to present a substantial and challenging piece of enhanced forum theatre, plus a host.
○ Working with colleagues gives reassurance and moral support when facing the classes, especially for the first time.
○ During the peer teaching, the classes will themselves need to be broken into smaller working sub-groups and there need to be sufficient peer teachers for each person to manage and supervise one of these.
○ Absences, either from planning or during the peer teaching sessions, can be covered.
○ The tasks of peer teaching can be shared and if a student falters at any time, there is somebody familiar with the plan who can pick up the thread and continue.
○ The pooling of ideas in planning is very important.
○ There is a 'critical mass' necessary for effective and energised work to be carried out, particularly in the planning phase.

Appropriate peer teaching group sizes per client group vary between three (at the very least) and seven. Fewer than three students will not provide the conditions above. More than six or seven students will make collaborative planning difficult. The number of students in the key class will determine the number of relay classes that can be used, and so on down.

Ratios should proceed on this numerical rule-of-thumb:

○ Key class
   Under 6 students: the program is probably not possible

6–9 students: one relay class

10–15 students: one or two relay classes

16 or more students: two or more relay classes.

○ First relay classes

Depending on how their own relay peer teaching is organised, the numbers may vary here. It is important to use the above ratios as a rule of thumb, and add to that considerations such as the logistics of travel to and from the primary school, and spaces for enhanced forum theatre, preparation and breakout.

○ Other relay classes

The same principles apply to any peer teaching that operates in the primary school – since the teacher is likely to be more actively involved with the class sub-groups in their planning and even peer teaching, the sub-groups should be of a size the teacher is comfortable with.

Organising the peer teaching

There is a major logistical issue to be decided when the program begins in a high school – how and where the peer teaching of the primary second relay class by the high school first relay class takes place. Schools have tried a number of models, all with some success, and both advantages and disadvantages. Geography may play a significant part, as may the particular dynamics and rhythms of the schools involved. If the high and primary schools are on the same campus, or nearby, it may be no major outing for the senior students to visit the primary school once or several times. For the primary students to visit the high school, or for either set of students to make a journey by transport, there is usually more at stake, and the visit or visits inevitably become more formal and ceremonial. A measure of ceremony or even festival adds a sense of occasion and reinforces the significance of the program.

The central drama technique

Enhanced forum theatre

CHAPTER 6

The origins of this complex amalgam of process drama and interactive theatre have been explained in Chapter 2, with the reasons why it has developed as the central teaching technique in *Cooling Conflict*. **Enhanced forum theatre** (or **EFT** as we shall call it here for convenience) is complex because bullying and conflict are complex, and oversimplifying real conflict is often why attempts to solve it come unstuck. However, the technique is quite straightforward to understand and manage for both school students and teachers unfamiliar with drama pedagogy. Just follow the steps, and the authentic structures of **conflict** and **bullying** will emerge in a recognisable form that allows students and teachers to actively experiment with **escalating** and **de-escalating** them, and this will invariably lead into valuable reflective and clarifying discussion.

Glancing ahead at the number of steps you are being asked to take may look daunting. However, most of these follow on quite naturally from each other and take much less time to put into practice than they do to explain in words . . . and once in practice, will be very much easier for the audiences to pick up when it is their turn to use them. The detail will help you the first time through, and then be quickly internalised. Everything in this chapter is manageable not only by non-Drama teachers, but also by groups of students, well down into the primary school years – with a little help from those teachers.

Each **EFT** play will dramatise a serious and unresolved conflict or ongoing bullying (which, remember, is defined earlier as the *continued* abuse of power, not an isolated incident). The actors will prepare and present the situation in three scenes, showing the *latent*, *emerging* and *manifest* stages of the conflict or bullying. The whole play is repeated, then parts of it, with the audience becoming involved in trying to **resolve** or at least **de-escalate** the situation. The audience will be involved in two ways: in direct and active participation,

intervening in the action, and in discussion leading to further scenes in the play. Not all the situations will be fully resolved. In fact, the better the EFT, the less likely it is to come to a totally 'happy ending' – but the students will end up with a very thorough understanding of all the dynamics and relationships involved, and be able to clearly identify the factors that tend to both escalate and de-escalate it. The play will be played in the classroom or drama space, without costumes, set or elaborate props, so the careful preparation of the play to be as clear as possible is crucial.

Steps 1–4 explain the creation and preparation of a piece of EFT, and Steps 5–8 explain how it operates.

Step 1: selecting the performing group or 'team'

The performing team, who will also devise the play, should consist of from five to eight people, all but one of whom will be actors. So in a large class of 30 students, there will be from four to six teams, each of which will devise a separate EFT play.

The team needs to be small enough for the students in it to be able to work together coherently, with everybody clearly aware of the whole play, but there need to be sufficient people to play the major roles in the three stages of the conflict. Some actors can double minor or bystander roles in different scenes, but it is inadvisable to have major parts doubled, since this will confuse the audience. (The play is presented without costumes or props, remember, and with the actors often playing parts entirely against their age, their character and their gender.)

The non-acting member needs to be a confident person capable of managing the leadership role of **host** or '**joker**' as the position is known in standard forum theatre (really just a Master of Ceremonies). These duties are described below. Depending on the chemistry of the class, the teams may be selected by the teacher, self-selected, or in the case of the **confessions** method of selecting a story (see Chapter 7 for a full description), team selection will happen automatically.

Step 2: selecting the story of conflict or bullying

The story needs to be complex enough to present the audience with a really difficult challenge, where right and wrong are not simplistically presented and all the characters have their own integrity and justification for their actions, where the behaviour is authentic to real life, and where the conflict can be seen to emerge in those three stages.

We recommend one of the following three methods for selecting the story.

Method 1: client stories

If the EFT plays are to be performed to an audience beyond the class itself, such as younger peers, then finding out some real stories of conflicts or bullying from that audience will obviously be authentic, though the original situations may need fleshing out, and they will certainly need fictionalising. The actors can find out from their potential audience what incidents of bullying or conflict have been troubling them by visiting the class – as recommended in Chapter 5 – and talking to the students, or administering a questionnaire which they can then look through to find an incident or combination of incidents that provide a relevant and arresting storyline.

Method 2: our stories

Another way of guaranteeing authenticity is to collect and choose a real-life story from the performing team. We strongly recommend the technique of **confessions** (see Chapter 7 for a detailed step-by-step explanation of this technique), which we have found to work equally well with all kinds of students, from primary ages to adult. **Confessions** is in its own right both great fun and very powerful emotionally and cognitively, and it has built-in emotional protections to ensure that the unfinished business from the original real conflict does not 'leak' into the classroom performance.

However the story is chosen, even more with 'our stories' than with 'client stories' it is imperative to fictionalise it, and flesh it out to the demands of the EFT three-scene structure.

Method 3: other people's stories

It is of course perfectly acceptable to start with a fictional story in the first place. The performing team will have plenty of experiences of conflict and bullying, theirs and other people's, to draw on, to devise a storyline that fits the EFT demands. Again, we recommend the 'headlines' technique as we have found this to be another entertaining and lively technique that generates rich and authentic storylines. If your time for generating the story is limited, about the quickest form of playbuilding is 'multiple role circle'. (Both these techniques are described in detail in Chapter 7.)

Authenticity can sometimes be a problem with entirely fictional stories, where students may be tempted to incorporate melodramatic or glamorous but unlikely ingredients. We have found this to be a real problem with stories taken from films, television or novels that the students have been engaged by – it is very hard for them to project themselves into the lives of the rich and famous, for instance, with any sense of reality; and too often, the characters of soap opera stories or novels are themselves too thinly conceived for the devisers to have any real idea of how they would act in a particular situation, so they need more fleshing out than they are worth. If the EFT is being devised by a relay class studying English or History, for instance, the story could even come from there – dramatising a conflict that happened in a novel the students are studying, or in for example a World War I conflict. If so, domestic conflicts that are close to the students' own experience and interests are most appropriate – for example a clash between a child who wants to join up and a parent who is opposed to it, or a soldier returning to find no jobs and an altered family relationship.

Step 3: fleshing out the storyline

Step 3a: role circle

Whichever of the three methods above is used, we recommend that when each team has decided on a basic storyline, they should do a drama exercise derived from process drama known as **role circle**. The more seriously and intently the group plays this game, the better their EFT scenario will be.

This has three purposes:

○ to flesh out the story, enrich it with new dimensions and perhaps new characters, and problematise it further – the more problematic, the more effective it will be as EFT
○ to reinforce the joint ownership of the story by the whole team
○ to fictionalise it – in the case of 'client stories' and 'our stories' – and ensure that all members of both performing team and audience are entirely protected from any real-life associations creeping in.

All the team members stand round in a circle (round the outside of their chairs is a good device for giving a ritual seriousness to the exercise), and in turn round the circle, each member adds one piece, and one only, of *fictional* information to the story. This should be a piece of tangible data, rather than suggestions about the characters' emotional state. Naturally it must be consistent with the story decided on (though it can certainly give it a new twist), and no member may contradict anything that another member has proposed. (If the story has been selected by the 'confessions' method, the member whose story this originally was should *not* add anything and cannot intervene to object to someone else's contribution.) At the end of the exercise, it will no longer be any one person's story, but will have become *our* story. A good variant of this exercise that invariably throws up interesting and striking details, is to ask all members to imagine themselves as one of the characters in the situation, but not one of the main characters in the conflict. Rather they should imagine themselves as someone who knows something of the conflict, or perhaps just knows one of the protagonists – a parent or sibling, a teacher or an old friend, or a local shopkeeper or school janitor. Then each team member offers their fictional detail in the first person as that character, announcing first who they are. These characters need not reappear in the play itself, but sometimes they can be useful.

Step 3b: consolidation

When every member has made their contribution, the team should be given the opportunity, briefly only, to discuss and review these new factors in the story, to ensure that they don't in fact contradict each other, nor make the story unmanageable or unauthentic. The team can veto up to two of the contributions, but no more than that, and only if the person who made that contribution agrees to the deletion. During this discussion, the team should ensure that all the following are quite clear:

- the dramatic context and setting
- who is/are the protagonist/s, or in the case of bullying, who is the bully, who the bullied and who the complicit bystanders
- the relationships of all the main characters seen or mentioned
- the motives of the key characters
- how the conflict or bullying escalated through the stages – from latent, through emerging, to manifest
- exactly what happened, and the main characters' most important actions and responses.

Step 4: devising the play

Now the team or teams devise their EFT play. The amount of time available for this will vary, but at the very least half an hour should be given, because they need to be complete and rehearsed enough for the actors to be able to repeat the scenes as exactly as possible, a number of times. The students may need some help, including the instructions given in Step 4a, and the younger they are, the more they will need.

Step 4a: 'writing' the play

The following instruction should be made clear – perhaps on the board or as a diagram.

○ There will be three scenes:

–Scene 1 – latent conflict or bullying, where the audience will see the causes of the problem, but as yet the characters are not in conflict

–Scene 2 – emerging conflict or bullying, where the audience will see the conflict or bullying starting, with some of the characters aware of what is happening

–Scene 3 – manifest conflict or bullying, where the conflict or bullying is plain for all to see, and the scene ends at a major crisis.

○ The '5 Ws' need to be clear to the audience in each scene: *what* is happening, exactly *who* is involved, *where* it is happening, *when* it is happening, and most important, *why* it is happening.

○ Each scene will be set at least one week apart – as described earlier, this is necessary to ensure that the conflict or bullying is substantial, sustained and hard to solve – young children in particular tend to conflate the three stages, sometimes into moments apart!

○ Each scene will include the bully, the bullied and at least one complicit bystander, or for other kinds of conflict, the protagonist and antagonist(s). Other characters may change between scenes, but the team must remember that this may include doubling of parts, so *who* they are must be made clear each scene.

○ The play must respect the story and if appropriate the contribution of the original story-teller by taking it seriously.

○ The action or the host's introduction must make clear what cannot be seen – such as the actual setting, and the gender, age and race of the characters – since there will be no scenery and minimal props and costumes, if any.

Step 4b: casting the play

The play is cast – students should normally be permitted and encouraged to play whatever parts they feel most comfortable with. One member of the team, the host, will not take an acting part – but can help to direct and provide a critical 'eye'. If the story of the play has emerged through 'Confessions', the team member whose original story is at the heart of this play should normally neither be the host, nor take the role of the character s/he originally played in real life (remind them that it is no longer his/her story, but a fiction).

Step 4c: producing the play

The students improvise and start rehearsing the three scenes. They should firstly be concerned with the *narrative*: making the story clear to the audience; making sure that everybody in the team knows who does what, and in what sequence; and getting the basic motivation of all the characters developed.

If there is time, step 4d should be included, but at the very least, the team must work out a basic motivation for all of their characters – this is very important in the performance. It needs to be stressed that even the bad guys have their own integrity, and a reason for doing what they are doing.

Props and costume should be very minimal, if any, and only used where they are significant to help the audience recognise a character, or if they have a symbolic significance to the action – the lunch-box that gets stolen, or a walking stick to denote an old person.

Scenery similarly should be minimal and schematic – you can usually manage with a few chairs and a table, that can double as furniture, beds, walls, windows. The actors should be encouraged to make whatever they do not have access to and so need to mime very clearly. Fewer stage props mean less time wasted scene-changing – remind them of this if necessary.

Fighting may well form a significant part of particularly Scene 3. The students must be reminded firstly to be careful towards each other, secondly to remember that the purpose is not just to be realistic but also to show the audience clearly what is happening and who is in control. A very good technique, if there is time, particularly if the class has some experience in drama, is to use a non-naturalistic technique, such as to go into slow-motion, or use a series of frozen 'snapshots' or **freeze-frames**. This stylised action can be controlled by the host, quite artificially. It also needs to be stressed to the actors, that this will only work if the non-naturalistic convention is quite clear and distinct – it needs to be exaggerated and unnatural. It may seem funny and the audience may well laugh, but curiously enough it will *not* destroy the tension, if the audience is believing in the authenticity of the storyline they are seeing. The actors just have to be in control of what they are doing, and do it confidently.

Step 4d (if time): backgrounding

The students should spend some time on **backgrounding** their characters, so that they understand not only what they are doing at all times, but why. This will be very important in the second performance of the EFT, when the audience will '**hot-seat**' some of the characters to discover their motives, and may also stop the action at any time to find out exactly what some of the characters are thinking. It should be stressed that the EFT will be more effective the harder it is to resolve, and the more human it is. Simple heroes, villains and victims will not make the play believable, and nor will the audience learn anything useful from it . . . and *that*, you can stress, is the team's very important purpose.

There are a number of techniques that may be helpful in **backgrounding** the characters:

○ *Profiling*: the teacher or leader may ask a series of questions to flesh out the background of *all* the characters, which each will answer for themselves, even possibly jot the answers down. These may relate to such things as: full name, exact age, family and sibling details, recent history, residence, socio-economic status (are you from a wealthy or poor home? – how wealthy or poor?), hobbies and pastimes, employment (where applicable), and pets.

○ *Creating a written profile*: the leader may provide a pro-forma for some or all of the questions above – this might be in the form of a 'police dossier record'.

○ *Hot-seating* some of the key characters, to make sure the character is believable and the actor convincing.

Step 4e: rehearsal

Time must be given for the team to rehearse the scenes sufficiently:

○ for the audience to be able to see and hear clearly everything that is going on, follow the narrative and identify the characters and their motivations

○ for the team to be able to repeat the scene virtually exactly, with the key moments and statements fixed – this is very important, as the team will be repeating the play at least three times, parts of it more.

This may be a very good point to re-iterate the importance of taking the story seriously, respectfully, and of people behaving normally (if emotionally in places) and so the actors need not ham-act, exaggerate the characters, nor play for laughs or effect.

Step 4f: preparing the host

The host must prepare his/her introduction, which sets the scene, for each of the three scenes, as economically as possible. Since there is no scenery, the exact locations of the scenes and the time of day when each scene takes place will probably need to be explained. Since there is no costume, and in all likelihood some of the actors will be playing a character of age, sex or cultural group different from themselves, the host may need briefly to introduce the characters (though obviously the clearer the exposition in Scene 1, the less will have to be explained). If possible, the host should get the chance to rehearse the introductions to the scenes. The team or the host should make sure that the play has a proper and appropriate title – and maybe a helpful title for each scene.

Step 5: the first performance

Now the actors are ready, and the performances can start.

Step 5a: organising the class

This depends on the purpose of the EFT. If the aim is for the team to take the EFT to an outside audience, say to use as the basis of their peer teaching, then each team will prepare to perform to their younger clients, where normally the whole class will be the audience of this first piece. The team may wish to start their encounter with their peers by some other form of drama or preparatory games or exercises, or some basic introduction about conflict (see Chapter 7 for details).

If the EFT is just for use within the class, then there are a number of possibilities.

○ Each group performs its EFT in turn, and carries out the whole scenario of follow-up, with the rest of the class as audience.

○ If time is limited and the class is well-controlled, then teams can be paired up to present their EFT with just one other team as audience. The teams take it in turns, and several plays will be performed simultaneously. Obviously this entails splitting the students into an even number of teams at the outset! So long as there is room for this to happen (and the noise may be considerable!) it works surprisingly well providing the leader or teacher can keep an eye on the groups, have a regulated time-frame that the groups are made aware of, and in particular keep an eye on helping out the host as necessary.

The first option is preferable, because it allows the teacher or peer teachers to observe and control the whole interaction. They can use the intervals in the performance to probe and problematise, asking questions to extend the audience's thinking and develop the reflective discussion that generates the most valuable learning of all.

Step 5b: setting up the performance space

This is quite simple (see the diagram in Appendix 2). The actors need a performance space large enough for them to carry out all the dramatic action clearly, and they should be encouraged to use space as expansively as the room permits. They need to know where their own entrance and exit points are, and how to denote this to the audience if there are no convenient doors or curtains (see below). They do not need a 'proper' stage or raised platform – in fact it is usually a disadvantage, setting up a formality that discourages audience participation. There needs to be space at the front, facing the audience for the '**hot-seat** chair' (see below, 'The second performance'). The audience should be arranged so that they can all see the action, and so that they can easily converse or discuss with each other – an arc of seats, one or two deep, facing the stage space, is ideal.

Step 5c: Let the show begin!

When the audience is seated, the host steps forward and introduces the play, setting the scene for 'Scene One – Latent conflict (or bullying)'.

The play is then performed throughout, without interruption, except from the host introducing the second and third scenes.

Step 6: the second performance

Step 6a: the host anchors the show

At the end of the first performance, the host steps forward to introduce the second performance, which is in two parts. S/he brings a chair right 'downstage' (close to the audience) and places it facing the audience. This is the hot-seat. The actors stand or sit in line 'upstage' (at the back). The host announces that the audience will be asked to help resolve the conflict or bullying, and in order to help them, the spectators can now find out more about the conflict, and what drives the characters, by two methods.

Step 6b: into the hot-seat

In the first of these, the host invites the audience to nominate which character they would most wish to talk to, in order to find out more about the conflict, its background, or the character's own motives. When the audience has reached a consensus or majority, the host instructs the actor to step into the hot-seat, still in **character**, and invites the audience to put questions – stressing that they need to be serious questions that might help in resolving the conflict (sometimes the audience just want to speak to the bully, to give him or her a piece of their mind, which is *not* the purpose of this activity, so should be discouraged!). The actor must answer the questions seriously, and not drop out of role. If faced with a question that has not been decided in advance, the actor must improvise a convincing fiction (and the other actors must listen and be ready to incorporate this).

Sometimes it may be in the character's nature to be evasive, or untruthful, or braggardly. If so, and the audience wishes (or is getting frustrated) the host can 'press the truth button', and then the character must respond truthfully to the questions, including revealing what s/he might wish to conceal.

Each hot-seat episode will probably take about five minutes (though the older the students, the longer and more absorbing it can be, with the actors invariably demonstrating quite unexpected depths of subtlety and convincing role-play). Depending how much time is available, it is useful to have up to three characters hot-seated, though more than that and the technique starts to pall.

A variant of this is to line all the characters up 'downstage' and invite the audience members to throw questions at any of them – with the constraint that they *will* answer truthfully. If this technique is used, the host should ensure that questions are directed at a specific character, who must answer, rather than at anybody. Moreover, the characters must not interrupt or get into improvised dialogue with each other. Generally we have found that this technique keeps the energy level high, but has less dramatic tension than the single hot-seat interrogation, and the audience gets much less depth of analysis.

It can easily be seen that the hot-seating works best, and the conflict is both most authentic and richest in learning possibilities, if the actors have had time to background their characters thoroughly, and can justify their actions and motives convincingly and consistently.

Step 6c: thought-tracking

After the hot-seating, the host announces that the play will be performed a second time, and this time the audience can get to find out exactly what any character was thinking at any key moment – **thought-tracking**. Any audience member can freeze the action at any time, just by calling out the word '**Freeze!**' The actors will immediately become immobile, and (through the host) the audience member can nominate a character. That character must then speak exactly what is going through his/her mind at that moment. The audience member can nominate more than one character, and when they have spoken their line or lines, the host re-starts the action, from the same point.

This technique may need a little practice in the rehearsal period, with the leader or teacher stressing that to keep it dramatic the words must be *direct speech, first person* and *immediate* (not 'well, I expect she would say something like . . .') – and if possible, more substantial than the very obvious one-worder or exclamation. Again, the more backgrounding that has been done, the more effective and revealing this technique is – and it is also a dramatic skill that certainly improves with practice.

Step 7: the third performance

By this time the audience is fully conversant with the whole sorry story and the nature and depth of the problem, and ready to have a go at resolving, or at least de-escalating it.

Step 7a: (optional) discussion groups

If the audience is very intent and beginning to discuss the situation among themselves already, or alternatively if they are very timid, it may be a good time to break them into small discussion groups, and invite each group to consider the three scenes of escalating conflict or bullying they have seen, and try to identify whether there were any points where one of the characters – any character, not just the main protagonists – might have acted differently, and de-escalated or resolved the conflict. This can be a useful discussion and provide the impetus for informed and intelligent intervention. However, the teacher(s), in consultation with the host, should use their judgment about whether that would diffuse the energy and focus, and they should proceed immediately to the third performance.

Step 7b: preparing for the intervention

The host announces that in the third performance, the audience will be invited to take a direct part in three ways. Firstly, they can **intervene** in the scene – they will become not spectators, but **spect-actors**; secondly, they must be '**magic**'-spotters (see Step 7c below), which will give them a significant control mechanism, along with the host; thirdly, they will find that they want to stop and discuss the action, and what has happened, and time will be made available for this. First, however, the host explains the rules of the interventions and in particular '**magic**'.

Step 7c: the forum performance

The play will be started as it has been twice before, but this time, as soon as a point is reached when any **spect-actor** believes that one of the characters might have improved the situation by acting differently, that spect-actor can call out '**Freeze!**', and the actors will freeze, as in the second performance. This time, however, the spect-actor will nominate the character who may be able to improve the situation by behaving differently. The spect-actor will then take the place of the actor who is in the role of that character. The scene will continue ad lib, with the spect-actor in role making the intervention and the other characters behaving according to their mood and personality, until one of three things happens – which the audience will immediately identify:

○ The intervention will be successful and the play will end naturally and happily, no doubt with a round of admiring applause for the successful spect-actor.

○ The intervention will not be successful, owing to the intransigence of some of the other characters, and that it is not the most appropriate intervention – quite often the interventions actually escalate the conflict! In this case, the host stops the action, often among a lot of amusement, and the spect-actor re-takes his or her place in the audience (with a rueful 'well-tried' or round of applause from the host and audience. This is important for the spect-actor not to feel a failure, even if the strategy failed). That may lead to spontaneous discussion among the audience, which should actually be encouraged, though the actors should *not* take part in this – and should be prevented by the host, if they try! Then the original actor steps back into character, the play re-starts at the point the action was originally frozen for the intervention, and it continues until the next call of 'Freeze!'

○ **Magic** will happen (or appear to happen), and either an audience member or the host will call out the magic word 'Magic!' and the action will again immediately freeze. 'Magic' in this context means that the action takes a turn for the unbelievable, and the play becomes untrue-to-life. There are two reasons this can happen (and usually does):

• because the intervening spect-actor is behaving in a way that is quite out-of-character or mood for the person whose role s/he has taken – say, the bully is smitten by repentance and offers reparation, or a diffident protagonist becomes unwontedly assertive, or

• because the spect-actor has introduced a way of resolving the problem, or a new piece of fiction, that is co-incidental, convenient and unlikely – e.g. a rich aunt has suddenly agreed to pay all the money back, or the bullied has just been selected for the Olympic athletic squad.

When the call of 'Magic!' is made, either by an audience member or the host, the host immediately instigates an audience discussion, with the person who made the call firstly explaining why s/he thinks the action is unauthentic, then other audience members giving their opinion whether it is or not. During all this, the actors are *not* allowed to participate, but must stay frozen, or at least still and in position – this is very important, to transfer some of the power of decision-making to the audience. If a consensus cannot be reached, the host calls for a vote. If the audience majority thinks the action is magic, then the spect-actor steps down (and is again thanked for a good try), and the action is re-started at the moment prior to the intervention. If the audience decides that the intervention is not magic, then the spect-actor is permitted to continue in the play from its latest point, until a resolution, or an escalation, or another call of 'Magic!'

If a spect-actor wishes to intervene at an earlier point than the action has reached – say the play has reached the manifest Scene 3 and a spect-actor has an idea of an intervention that might have been made in Scene 2, it is up to the host to decide whether to allow the action to be 're-wound' or not.

Eventually, the play will come to a finish, or be cut. The host, and the teacher/leader(s), need to be keeping a careful eye on the audience's energy, attention and interest levels, and cut the play before it becomes wearisome. There may well be no resolution or even de-escalation, as in real life, when the play is cut. If the EFT scenarios are well-devised and complex, there will very rarely be a clear-cut resolution. That is certainly true to life, where conflicts are rarely solved by intervening at moments of confrontation – these may be the worst points at which to try, and escalation is a much more likely result. Since it is not the purpose of this technique to train the students in bad conflict management techniques, this point sets the scene well for Step 8, in preparation for which a reflective discussion led by the teacher or the host is probably necessary at this point.

In truth, the forum embodies much more than the performance itself, and the most important learning about conflict and bullying often comes as it is made explicit in reflective discussion, which can get quite heated. Therefore, subject to the inevitable constraints of time, the opportunities for discussion should be maximised, particularly at the places above, where we have identified standard openings – rather than pressing on with the performance. After all, the tension of wondering how it will end is a very powerful one that will usually sustain the interest in the on-going play, even while the audience is interrupting it with discussion.

During these interventions, there may be quite a lot of laughter – in particular when somebody is ambushed by the call of 'Magic', or one of the interventions breaks down, or somebody unwittingly says something very 'magic' or melodramatic or corny. There can often be a real outburst of mirth that may even briefly cause the actors to break role and join in. Although this is a slight interruption to the continuity of the piece and certainly breaks the tension, it is actually a very healthy sign, signalling cognitive recognition of what is or is not real, and also the release of pent-up feelings. So the host's or teacher's natural instinct to repress the laughter is actually misplaced (except in very occasional circumstances, when there can be an element of cruelty about it – which then provides meat for a discussion).

If the actor chosen to be the host is very young, timid or unassertive, it will invariably be necessary for the teacher to take on some of the role of host and support him or her – whilst still leaving the host with some responsibility and autonomy in running the encounter.

Step 8: Scene Four – hors de combat

Now comes what is likely to be the most important and useful part of the whole epic: **Scene Four**.

After letting the forum performance demonstrate that there are *no* easy or immediate answers to that conflict or bullying scenario, the host, or the leader/teacher, divides the audience into sub-groups of five to six students. The host explains that this conflict or bullying is clearly too difficult to solve on the spot. What would happen in real life is that some mediation is needed 'off the battlefield'. Just as in adult domestic brawls it is standard police procedure for the combatants to be separated and spoken to apart, so here perhaps somebody could act as a mediator, and talk separately to at least one of the protagonists, to cool them down and get their help in resolving the conflict or the on-going bullying. Each sub-group is asked to decide and nominate:

- ○ which protagonist would be best or most appropriate to 'target' for mediation?
- ○ who might be best placed to act as mediator – who else might have the motivation and the means to have an influence on one of the protagonists in the conflict? This may be one of the less involved parties that we have met on stage; it might be somebody mentioned in the scenario, such as the parent or brother or sister of a protagonist. If nobody likely is suggested, then it might be a more detached or professional mediator, such as a teacher or counsellor.
- ○ where and when would be a good opportunity for this party to try and mediate with the protagonist?
- ○ how would that party start this mediating process?

In addition, the spect-actors' sub-group should:

- ○ nominate one member from their group to take on the role of that mediator
- ○ discuss and decide the strategy for addressing the conflict.

Then in turn each group announces their proposed context for mediation and these are discussed and compared by all the audience. Then whichever suggestions are decided on as likely to de-escalate the conflict, those groups are invited to try out their proposal. The members of each group help the actors to set up the space appropriate to their proposed encounter. The group's nominee then plays out this scene with the chosen actor(s), whose task as the protagonist is to respond in role, but make it as difficult as possible (but just possible) for the strategy to work. Again, the audience watches the action, ready to call 'Magic!' if either actor bends probability too far.

The two audience participation techniques from the second performance (Step 6) – **hot-seating** and **thought-tracking** – can be used to enhance this Scene Four. During the scene, any member of the audience may call 'Freeze!' and request a hot seat for someone, or thought-tracking of the moment.

The chosen Scene Four may involve several of the protagonists, whom the audience group believes might be able to resolve the conflict without outside intervention, but in some setting away from the battleground. In this case the scene can be set up just with the original actors, briefed by the group. The actors themselves can be free to call 'Magic!' if the terms of their briefing include behaviour they deem improbable or out of character.

Step 9: reflection

One of the sub-groups' scenarios may provide a satisfactory resolution, and they don't all have to be tried – this is very time-consuming, and can become tedious. Usually one or other finishes in some lively discussion, which can be led by the host or the leader/teacher. It may often be sufficient in itself, as valuable as pursuing the enactments to a contrived resolution. In any case it is valuable to finish the forum with a reflective discussion exploring other moments of possible, better intervention; or whether this conflict would or could ever be fully resolved; or even following the breakdown to look at possible consequences if the conflict was not well-handled. The discussion stimulated by the performance is often the major learning outcome.

Enhanced forum theatre

Forum scene – latent bullying.

Forum scene – manifest bullying.

Forum – I'll play the bullied: a spect-actor intervenes.

Forum – the spect-actor fronts the bully.

enhanced forum theatre

An extraordinary piece of enhanced forum theatre was performed by a group of Year 9 first relay class students to the rest of their class as the outcome of their work on the *Cooling Conflicts* program. Although the key group of Year 11 and 12 students initially assisted the Year 9s in developing the piece, in performance it was all their own work, except for the role of host, which was taken by one of the key group senior drama students.

Their EFT play was based on the experiences of Tranh, a Vietnamese girl in the group. She had described how she arrived at a new school in the middle of the year and was victimised because of her poor spoken English. Tranh told the story but did not want to act in it nor contribute to its development. Her reluctance to perform or be a leader was characteristic of the other Vietnamese students in the class, particularly the girls. However, once the rest of the group started dramatising the story, Tranh stepped in actively, correcting the mistakes they were making and directing the action.

When developing forum theatre it is vital to background the story as Tranh did for the actors in her story. In this way the context of the performance will have authenticity. It is equally important for the actors to background their own characters to give them genuine motivations for their actions, rather than just presenting them as the heroes or villains of the piece. All the characters in forum theatre must be represented with integrity if the work is to be valuable in conflict management.

When Tranh's story was performed as EFT for the rest of the class, there were a number of interventions from the audience, none of them successful, until a final, ingenious attempt by a student de-escalated the conflict with extraordinary effectiveness.

Tranh's story

The host introduces the story and the characters involved, and sets the scene in the classroom. The audience is instructed to watch the play through very carefully without interruption. At the end of each scene the host introduces the next scene, describing the time, place and stage of conflict.

Scene One: latent conflict

The play begins with the teacher in the story introducing Tranh to her new class. A number of students mock her attempts at spoken English and two girls in particular, Libby and Tasha, tease her throughout the lesson. Tranh does not respond.

Scene Two: emerging conflict

A few days later after school, Libby and Tasha catch Tranh in the playground and begin to tease her, trying to make her say words she is unable to pronounce such as 'Sorry'. Again Tranh does not respond. The girls begin to call her names and physically bully her, pulling her hair and pushing her around. A group of Vietnamese boys arrive to help Tranh and Libby and Tasha run away.

Scene Three: manifest conflict

In the classroom the next day, Libby and Tasha have hidden some rotting fruit in Tranh's desk. When Tranh opens her desk, the smell is overpowering. The teacher blames Tranh and the two girls call out insults suggesting that Tranh always eats rotten food. The teacher hears and orders Tranh to tell her what is going on with Libby and Tasha. Tranh tells her about the bullying and the teacher sends the two girls to the Principal. As they leave they tell Tranh she is dead meat. When the lesson finishes and Tranh exits the girls are waiting for her.

Freeze

This was the end of Tranh's story. The host invited the audience to hot-seat any character to clarify the story. One boy asked Tranh herself what had happened next and she answered that she had been beaten up, the three of them had been sent to the office and the bullying had continued until the ring leader, Libby, had left the school.

The host instructed the actors to perform the play again, without interruption, and asked the audience as they were watching to try and identify places at each stage of the conflict where they could intervene as one of the characters to de-escalate the conflict.

The play was performed again without interruption.

A **role circle** or **thought-tracking** could have been used effectively here to discover more about how the girls involved in the conflict felt about the situation. The involvement of other people such as parents and teachers could also have been explored by using a role circle at this point.

The host instructed the actors to perform once more, but this time asked members of the audience to call out 'stop' when they wanted to intervene. She reminded the audience that they could intervene as any character in the play and if they belatedly recognised a place where they could have intervened after the moment had passed, they could stop the action and request a rewind back to that moment.

The play began again and in the second scene in the playground a boy intervened, taking the role of one of the Vietnamese boys who had rescued Tranh. In this role he pursued Libby and Tasha and told them if they ever touched Tranh again his gang would get them. The actors playing Libby and Tasha were briefly nonplussed, but then decided they would go home and phone up all the Australian boys they knew to get them to come to school to fight the Vietnamese boys.

There were laughter and cheers from the audience at this clever piece of improvisation and everyone agreed when the host suggested that this intervention had actually made the conflict much worse. The play then proceeded to the end with no further interventions.

The host asked if anyone had thought of another intervention and a girl put her hand up. Scene One was run again and the girl took the role of Tasha and told Libby that she should stop teasing Tranh as it wasn't fair. There were shouts of 'Magic' from the audience and all agreed with the host that this was completely implausible.

The play continued and in Scene Three a boy intervened to take the role of the teacher and after the rotten food incident sent Libby and Tasha home with a note for their parents. The girls still waited for Tranh outside the school gate. The host asked if the intervention was worthwhile and the audience agreed it was but pointed out that it did not work.

At this point thought-tracking could have been requested again and each of the characters, Libby, Tasha and Tranh asked their thoughts during the confrontation outside the school gate. This would have clearly established that the conflict had been escalated by the teacher and not resolved.

Next a girl asked for a re-wind to the moment after the rotten food incident. She took the role of teacher and separated Libby and Tasha, forcing Libby to sit with Tranh. Both Libby and Tranh objected violently. The teacher told them that they would be forced to sit together until they could get on. Libby again threatened to kill Tranh, blaming her for the teacher's action.

At this stage another girl intervened to take the role of Tranh. This was the first time this had happened in the forum. In role as Tranh the girl offered a deal to Libby – they would pretend to get on in front of the teacher and once the teacher was convinced and separated them, they could be enemies again. Tranh and Libby shook on the deal, to cheers and applause from the audience.

In the discussion, a few of the audience claimed this was magic, but most disagreed, seeing Tranh's offer as a very clever piece of conflict management and Libby's response as believable in the circumstances. Whether the conflict would resume again was hotly debated, but the clear de-escalation was generally acknowledged.

Extension: beyond the forum

The class took this particular piece of forum theatre no further. However, the kinds of interventions they practised, while they made for an entertaining and thought-provoking exercise, were not entirely authentic. It would have been appropriate to use Scene Four in Tranh's story to see if a long-term and realistic solution was possible in this story of conflict and bullying.

This piece of enhanced forum theatre very clearly illustrates how effectively it can be used to explore cultural conflict and bullying relevant to students. It also demonstrates just how students can experiment with management strategies to increase their own skill in managing conflicts.

Drama in the program
Enhancements and enrichments

CHAPTER 7

Introduction

Although enhanced forum theatre is the key drama technique in the *Cooling Conflict* program there are a number of other techniques and activities that are designed to enhance and enrich the use of drama in the program.

The first set of these are methods of playbuilding that provide interesting and challenging ways of developing the bullying and conflict situations and characters that provide the content of enhanced forum theatre.

Secondly, this chapter provides a series of drama activities and exercises designed to warm up the students to participate in the drama. These activities also focus the attention and concentration of the students on the situations and characters they are exploring.

Finally, community theatre in education provides an enrichment of the program that has the potential to take the program beyond the school and into the whole community.

Playbuilding for enhanced forum theatre

1. Confessions

This is the recommended technique for developing enhanced forum theatre for *Cooling Conflict*. The technique starts with the participants' real-life stories of unresolved conflict and bullying, to make sure there is a basic authenticity. However, this raw story is then fictionalised and elaborated, to make it safe for the story's real-life protagonist, to give all the actors in the group ownership of the story and to develop a forum play that is dramatically tense and complex to resolve. Like the steps for EFT, this technique takes quite a few words to spell out in detail, and so may look complicated and daunting at first, but in action it is clear, easy to follow and to manage.

Step 1: confessional pairs

Step 1a: organising the group

The class or performing group is broken up into pairs. It is preferable for the pairs not to know each other too well; best-friend couples will have more difficulty with the exercise than comparative strangers, so a mixing-up exercise may be used. Each pair is then asked to find a space together away from other pairs and designate themselves as A and B. This first task is best done seated on chairs facing each other. Each pair is then asked to think of a real conflict or ongoing bullying episode from their own life, that has left 'unfinished business' – that is, that has never been satisfactorily resolved. This may be from the present, the recent or distant past. Participants must be warned that this must not be a conflict:

○ that involves others within this class or performing group, or
○ where the emotions are so raw that the telling or disclosure might be upsetting or traumatic for them since these stories will be played with and altered.

Step 1b: mirror, mirror

A is first asked to tell his or her story of conflict or bullying to B, as fully as s/he can within about two or three minutes – giving the context and as much detail as possible. B must listen carefully and respectfully and on no account interrupt, until A has finished, when B can ask any clarifying questions, if there is time. All the As then tell their stories to their B simultaneously.

After two or three minutes, when the leader decides the stories are completed, B is then instructed to re-tell the same story that s/he has just heard – A's story, as completely as possible, but *in the first person* as if the story had happened to B (no matter that there might be factors of age, geography, gender or culture that would make it impossible; B's task is to empathise with the story and tell it completely convincingly). A must listen, and must on no account interrupt, no matter what mistakes are being made, until the end, when s/he can compliment or correct B as appropriate. Again, the leader gives about three minutes.

Step 1c: refracting mirror

Both members of the pairs are asked to put A's story to one side for the time being – but not forget it. B now gets the chance to tell his or her own story to A. The rule is the same, though to add a little spice, the participants may be warned that a new rule will be introduced after B has told the story. As before in reverse, B now relates his or her story to A, in detail and with care.

Once again, A prepares to re-tell B's story *in the first person* as if it had happened to A, with the following optional addition, at the teacher's discretion. This time, B will also take a step into fiction, and as they listen, they will take the role of a very good friend, counsellor or confidant of A, and at the end, A will discuss 'my problem' with B and ask advice. If this elaboration is used, a couple of extra minutes need to be allotted for that discussion, where B and A earnestly try and solve A's problem (which was of course actually B's!).

Step 2: sharing the stories

Each pair is now asked to decide on one only of these stories to continue with – perhaps the one that is most tangled and hardest to resolve. The pair is going to tell the story together – each member will tell half the story, but both still in the first person as if it were their own. The pairs are given a minute to arrange their stories, then the pairs are brought together into larger groups, with the members sitting in a circle, but next to their partner. Groups of four pairs (eight people) are absolutely ideal, though it could be three or five. For the sake of timing this step, it is best if all the groups are the same size. These groups will later on each become a performing group for the enhanced forum theatre.

In turn, each pair tells its chosen story to the rest of the new group, in detail and with care as before. All the groups do this simultaneously. It is more fun if the group does not know whose story it originally was, so that they have to guess according to the effectiveness and sincerity of the telling. At the end, normally this should be revealed (perhaps after a vote!). However, if the pair for some reason does not wish to reveal whose story it was, this should be respected. This step must be given sufficient time – for four stories, 15–20 minutes is necessary. The leader should monitor the groups' progress.

Step 3: deciding the group story

When all the stories have been told, each group then has to decide which one they will use as the basis of the EFT. This story will be added to and changed by the group, and taken out of the hands of the original 'owner' of the story. However, they should choose a story that is as difficult as possible to resolve, and one that has a large number of complications – involving more than two or three people. The next step is to give the protagonist a new and fictional name – from now on it is no longer the story of the original A or B.

Step 4: making the story communal

The final step in this preliminary play-building process is quite crucial, and is an important step to enrich the story, to 'give the whole group ownership of the story' and also safeguard the original teller, who will no longer 'own the story'; that is to play the exercise **role circle** (see Chapter 6, Step 3a on page 96). This will add germane fictional elements to the conflict story to further problematise it, help each member of the group to feel they have contributed to the story, and turn it into a new story of conflict that cannot be identified with any individual in the class, but is relevant to all.

2. Headlines

This is a quite different method of building and developing student-devised plays that is also useful for devising EFT for *Cooling Conflict*. It is particularly useful where there are barriers or inhibitions within the group that might inhibit the more personal disclosure of 'Confessions'. However, leaders should note that because the material starts with a more 'distanced' approach, the scenarios that arise are sometimes less immediately authentic, and the leaders may need to use fleshing out techniques such as **role circle** and **hot-seating** not only in the performance but in the devising.

Step 1: thematic brainstorm

The teacher divides the class into groups of about six and asks each group to decide on a theme that is problematic and involves conflict that all the class is, to a degree, interested in. This is better done with speed (say give the group one minute only) and the teacher may prefer to give them a common theme. Each group is asked to appoint a 'narrator/scribe'.

Step 2: newshounds

Each group is to quickly identify *a specific incident* incorporating manifest conflict that encapsulates whatever is problematic about the theme and is newsworthy. This incident should be left as bald as possible (it is very important that the incident *not* be filled out and backgrounded more than a minimum). The group has three tasks:

○ To write the first paragraph of a newspaper report about the incident – tabloid style if possible.

○ To find a juicy headline that encapsulates the incident's significance.

○ To prepare a 'news photo' (a **freeze-frame** or tableau) of a particularly sensational or problematic moment in the incident that illustrates the issue or the conflict. This can include the entire group except the scribe.

Again, the teacher should give the group just enough time to do this and write their paragraph – no more than 15 minutes.

Step 3: interrogating the images

The teacher focuses on one group at a time and stresses that in this step, the audience is more important than the performers. The group is asked to set up and be prepared to hold their 'news photo' for a long time while the scribe reads the headline and paragraph. The audience is to think of whatever questions this incident makes them want to ask. Usually it is a good idea to repeat the reading and display. Then, with the group still frozen (and not able to respond) the audience asks all their questions, giving the scribe time to write them all down. It may be helpful for the leader to paraphrase these and possibly to lead off the questioning. The questions will usually start by being simple narrative details (such as 'Who is that person?', 'What is she doing?') They should then start to dig deeper (for example, 'When he goes home tonight, what will he tell his wife?', 'Why was the child by herself?'). Again, the teacher may provide useful modelling. The group is not allowed to reply, even if they have a reply. The teacher should explain that this is because the audience questions may lead to a more fruitful possibility than their original scenario.

Each group in turn goes through the same process, so that all end up with a list of questions about their incident.

Step 4: selecting the focus

Each group is asked to identify a single question from their list that (a) interests them, (b) is clearly problematic, and (c) would shed light on the roots of this conflict, if investigated. They are instructed to identify a particular character who would be central to this question; that is, the question could not be answered without knowing more about this character. This person will be the *protagonist*. The next two stages may be done in either order depending on the leader's purpose:

4a The teacher asks the group to identify a time, earlier in the context, when the conflict was either latent or brewing, then ask them to devise and rehearse an improvised scene which features the protagonist and is a key moment in escalating the conflict to the next stage.

4b   The teacher instructs the group to background the protagonist very thoroughly; to avoid taking up judgmental positions and to try to create an authentic and consistent character. As soon as possible, the group members should 'hot-seat' each other. (Members of the group take turns role-playing the character, while the others fire questions at him/her.) The leader may like to suspend the group-work after a while to let a volunteer from each group be hot-seated by another group.

Step 5: selecting an incident

This depends on the leader's purposes. The groups may show their scene and the original 'later' incident and then vote on which incident all the class will now concentrate on, either to explore it further as process drama or as a playbuilt play for production. Alternatively, any or all of the group contexts can form the bases for EFT by each group.

3. Multiple role circle

This is a quick and enjoyable method of developing a fictional conflict or bullying situation. The story that emerges may need more fleshing out and elaborating than either 'confessions' or 'headlines'. However, it is a useful technique particularly for younger children, or those who have little experience of drama, or if time for preparation is limited.

For success, however, it does depend on the leader's effective questioning, and the active intelligence and generosity of the group or class. It will usually therefore need a few 'practice goes' before a usable or believable scenario emerges.

There is really only one step to this technique, which can be played as a game. It is in any case an excellent dramatic warm-up game to get a group focused and alert.

The whole class stands round in a circle, with the teacher or peer teacher in the middle. The teacher explains that there is really only one rule: that all players must accept the 'truth' of what has gone before, and so no responses may contradict that. This means listening carefully, and remembering what everybody else has said! The group is going together to invent a story of conflict or bullying – it may be the story of a bullied person or a bully, of somebody likeable or not, but the group's aim is to keep it as believable as possible (so the game needs to be taken seriously). Anybody may be questioned at any time, and they must answer immediately and in the first person.

The leader starts by asking a person at random to think of a name that is not their own – it can be either sex or any cultural group, then formally starting the 'interrogation' with:

What's your name?

If the answer is, for example,

My name is Michelle

the teacher turns to somebody else and says:

How old are you, Michelle?

and the respondent must answer immediately, with a reasonable age between ten and seventy. The next question, to a third random respondent, will probably be:

Where do you live, Michelle? [with the teacher constantly repeating the name, to remind the group that they must answer as this fictional character].

When some basic information has been established ('Who do you live with?'; 'How long have you lived there?') the leader should put in a leading question that will establish a context for the conflict. A few good leading questions are:

What were you doing down at the shopping mall last Friday evening?

How much did you see of the fight in the school yard last Thursday lunchtime?

Weren't you one of the people around outside the school gates at [such and such a time]?

From then on, the answers will dictate the next question, with the teacher like a detective, not supplying information, but trying to lead the players to develop the story from the protagonist's point of view, to find more background on the protagonist. Gradually a picture of a person, and a conflict situation, will emerge, and be fleshed out – how well will depend on the skill of the detective, and the level of effective contribution from the group. The teacher should ensure that the questioning incorporates everybody in the group before the game is cut – some people might have a second or third turn, to keep them on their toes.

The teacher decides when is an appropriate time to cut the game, and asks the group's opinion as to whether the character and situation are believable and likely.

It is unlikely that the very first attempt will provide a very memorable or usable scenario, since this is a game where the players improve very much with practice. The leader will probably need to have several dummy runs, during which s/he can point out the skills to aim for:

○ Firstly, some answers are better than others: for example, to the question 'have you always lived at home?', 'No, I had three years with my auntie' is likely to provide more interesting possibilities than 'Yes'.

○ The best answers are those that add something interesting but entirely believable: 'Could you see who was struggling?' 'Not exactly, I was behind the police officer, but I definitely saw somebody running away.'

○ Some answers actually block the development of the story: to 'What did you see in the school yard at lunchtime today' the answer 'Nothing' is unlikely to be very helpful (certainly from beginners, though to sophisticates of the game, it can suggest a dishonest protagonist and an interesting new struggle!).

○ The answers that block most unhelpfully are those that are made for effect, or to be clever or witty: 'What's your name?' 'Silly Solly.' 'Where did you live before you came to Brisbane?' 'Timbuktu.'

If the group is having difficulty getting started or grasping the game, the leader can usefully start with 'We are going to find out all about a person who has serious problems, and what those problems have led to'.

The players will probably keep the context very close to home to begin with: 'I'm fifteen'; 'I live in Brisbane.' For the purposes of EFT, this is actually a good thing, though it may seem to restrict the imaginativeness of the game. After all, it is fun in some ways to branch out, and sometimes very useful for developing the imagination – that answer of 'Timbuktu' could actually, if treated seriously, bring in a whole new multicultural context. However, in *this* context where the game is being used as a technique for developing enhanced forum theatre, the more recognisable and understandable the context is, the more authentic the resulting story is likely to be.

If the group is experienced and confident in drama, or already experienced at this particular technique, it is a good idea to hand the circle leadership over to a confident student from within the group. In any case, students who have practised the game themselves quickly become adept at leading it skilfully with their younger peers.

Warm-up games and group activities

1. Forming groups

Same/sequence game

1. Go around the class giving each student a number up to four in sequence. Ask the students to form their *same* groups – that is, all the number 1s together, 2s together, 3s together and 4s together.

2. In their *same* groups, tell the students to make four different shapes.

   –a *circle*, where they hold hands in a circle

   –a *star*, where they remain in a circle holding hands but turn their backs to the centre of the circle and stretch out, making the shape of a star

   –a *stretch*, where they hold hands in a straight line and stretch the line

   –a *scrum*, arms around each others shoulders in a huddle.

3. Now get the students to form their *sequence* groups, so that each group of four has numbers 1, 2, 3 and 4 in it.

4. In their *sequence* groups, get the students to practise making the different shapes – circle, star, stretch and scrum.

5. Now have a competition, calling out different group types, either '*same!*' or '*sequence*' and different shapes – e.g. 'same circle!', 'sequence star!', 'sequence stretch!', 'same scrum!'. The winners each time are the students who get into the right type of group and form the right shape first.

6. Repeat the competition a few times and then ask the students to sit down in their *same* or *sequence* groups depending on the size of groups you wish to work with.

Clumps

1. Ask the students to form groups of four to six.
2. Tell the groups to make a particular shape such as a pineapple, a horse, a jet ski, a tadpole.
3. Ask them to form another group which does not include anyone from their first group, or only one or two people depending on numbers.
4. Get them to form a different shape from the first group.
5. Repeat the exercise two or three times.

Body parts

1. Ask the students to walk around the room and touch hands with someone else.
2. Repeat the exercise a couple of times, in turn touching elbows, knees, fingers, backs, etc. Each time the students must make contact with someone different.
3. Now tell the students to touch elbows in groups of three, with students they have not contacted so far.
4. Now tell them to touch hands or knees in groups of four with students they have not contacted so far.
5. Start work with them in their groups of four.

2. Building focus

Relaxation

1. Ask the students to lie on the floor and close their eyes.
2. Tell the students to take a deep breath in, and as they breathe out to relax their arms. Repeat the instruction for the arms and then twice each for the back and the legs.
3. Ask them to breathe in up to a count of five, hold the breath and then breathe out quietly. Count for them two or three times and then instruct them to continue the breathing for themselves.

Visualisation

1. Do the relaxation breathing first.
2. Ask the students to imagine they are lying on a warm beach. Tell them to sense the sun on their faces, to hear the sound of the water lapping on the shore and to see the sail of a boat out to sea and to feel the sand under their bodies. (Alternatively, suggest another peaceful physical context.)

Circle of attention

1. Ask the students to sit still, close their eyes and do the relaxation breathing.
2. Tell them to open their eyes and focus on a single spot on the floor or wall in front of them.
3. Instruct them to widen the focus to take in everything within a metre circle around the spot.
4. Now ask the students to widen their circle of attention to take in the whole room.

3. Movement warm-ups

Mirror movement

1. In pairs the students sit facing each other and choose who is A and who is B.
2. A acts as the person and B as the mirror. A begins by moving only one hand whilst B mirrors this hand movement. A then begins to move both hands at the same time while B mirrors as closely and as simultaneously as possible.
3. A and B swap roles but this time standing up. B begins by moving one hand, then both, then some whole body movements such as miming getting dressed or playing a sport. A mirrors all the actions.

4. Now B stands behind A whilst A moves around the room miming different movements. B attempts to shadow A's movements.

Frozen sculptures

1. Working in pairs, one student freezes and is sculpted into different shapes by the partner. Swap.
2. Ask the pairs to create a series of images as freezes, giving them titles such as *Trapped, The Pickpocket, Disco Dancers, The Rescue, The Dinosaur*. Count down from five to one, then call Freeze! and ask them to hold the frozen image for a few seconds.
3. Pairs create a five second piece of movement entitled *The Accident*, which begins and ends with a freeze.

Machines

1. Form groups of six to eight and give each member of the group a number. Number One stands in the centre of the group and begins to make a machine-like movement.
2. Number Two joins on to Number One physically and picks up the machine movement and extends it.
3. One by one the other members enter in turn and add onto the shape and movement of the machine until the entire group is part of it.

4. Improvisations

Creating objects

1. With students working in pairs, ask one to mime the use of an object. The partner has to identify the object and then mime using it.
2. In pairs, one student sculpts an imaginary statue. The partner mimes making changes to the statue. The first student then mimes adding to the revised statue. The partner makes further changes to the enlarged statue. The partners describe to each other what they visualised as they sculpted and altered the statue.

Creating scenes

1. Working in groups of four to five, the students form a circle. One member of the group steps into the centre of the circle and takes up a posture or mimes doing something.
2. A second member enters the circle and adds to the improvisation through movement

and/or conversation. The other members of the group continue the process, adding to the scene until all members are involved.

Space jump

1. As in creating a scene above, one member of a group enters the circle and starts the improvisation by saying or doing something.
2. This time when the second member of the group enters, he or she tries to totally change the action and location of the improvisation. For example, the first student may lie down and mime sunbathing on the beach. The second student rushes in as a paramedic at a road accident and tries to revive the first student.
3. Each member enters in turn changing the action and location until all are involved.
4. They then exit in reverse order and as each one exits the improvisation reverts to the previous action and scene until the original student is left alone in the circle.

5. Characterisation

Character walks and talks

1. Tell the students to walk around the room taking on the body shape and movement of different characters as you name them – for example, a blind person, a very young child, a soldier, an elderly person, a shy person, a police officer, someone vain.
2. When you call out 'Talk!', they must begin talking to the person nearest to them in the character they have created in movement.

Bus stop

1. In groups one after another the students take on a character and walk up to a marked spot which is the bus stop and wait for the bus.
2. In character they must wait in the queue and talk to each other.

Emotion memory

1. Tell the students to lie down and take them through the relaxation exercise above.
2. Ask them to remember something really exciting that happened to them when they were younger, such as a party or Christmas or the Easter Show.
3. Get them to re-enact the experience, trying to recapture the authentic excitement.

4. Repeat the relaxation and memory recall, this time remembering something frightening and ask them to improvise a situation where an adult character is in a frightening situation. The students enact the situation as the adult, trying to find the authentic emotion.

Community theatre in education

This phase of *Cooling Conflict* follows the peer teaching phases and empowers the students to lead the bullying and conflict management agenda not only within the school, but also into the school's neighbourhood and wider community.

In this phase, the drama work turns to performance, to creating a play for a public audience and one that also involves the audience in active participation derived from forum theatre and process drama. This kind of theatre is known as **theatre in education** (TIE).

Either key or upper relay classes can carry out this phase with a range of audiences. It is advisable for the teacher(s) intending to implement this phase to have some drama teaching or at least practical theatre experience.

Like all public performance, it involves time-consuming preparation and rehearsal – some of it possibly in extra-curricular time. It may involve travel and some production costs and, particularly during the performance week, some timetable adjustments (according to the nature of the community being targeted). The benefits are:

○ to the audiences – in entertaining and thought-provoking presentation of bullying and conflict issues by their 'own' young people presented with both sincerity and energy

○ to the performers – like the peer teaching, the work involved in devising and presenting the performance reinforces their learning and understanding. The work also automatically carries the many other widely recognised benefits of devising and producing a public theatrical production

○ to the school – which can be seen to be living its mission and leading the community in developing harmony and cultural understanding.

Ideally a term's work in one subject should be devoted to this, which is Phase Four of *Cooling Conflict*.

The project can be broken into three periods:

○ Period 1: research and devising – 3–4 weeks
○ Period 2: rehearsal and production – 5–6 weeks
○ Period 3: performance and reflection – 1 week.

Period 1: devising

Step 1: identifying the context and audience

The first step – and the first lesson – is to discuss with the students what problematic bullying and cultural issues exist within the local community (and sub-communities) beyond the school. These can be discussed in the conflict management terms with which the students are now familiar, of looking at clashes of *interests, rights* and *power*, where assumptions and **stereotyping** prevent a harmonious co-existence and lead to *latent, brewing* or *manifest conflict.*

Where bullying is the focus, the imbalance of power in a situation becomes a key issue. Students should by now be familiar with the nature of the involvement of the 3Bs – the bully, the bullied and the bystander – in any bullying situation.

At this time, an appropriate audience can be canvassed. This should be an audience of people with some stake in the bullying or conflict issue being identified, likely to be approachable for the purposes of research and likely to be interested in attending a performance by the students to raise and examine the issues.

In one research project school, some of the possible audiences that the key class seriously considered, after identifying potential conflict issues, included:

○ other students their own age from neighbouring schools
○ senior citizens
○ police officers and families
○ local primary schools
○ parents
○ the local indigenous community
○ the local ethnic communities
○ motor cycle clubs
○ football clubs
○ hospital nurses.

Eventually they settled on the first, to concentrate on the conflict issues between parents and school leavers. Although it was not explicitly identified at this stage, inter-cultural ethnic conflict raised its head in the research period and was incorporated into two of the four stories that were interwoven in the final play.

It is important not to let this discussion drag on, but to make a majority or consensus decision at the end of the lesson.

Step 2: research

The students then become researchers and consult with the communities involved, to find raw material that is germane to the bullying or conflict issue identified and to create interest in the production. This usually means visits to become familiar with the community context and how it operates, interviewing key citizens, holding discussion groups with others . . . and keeping their eyes and ears open. Getting personal stories is usually the richest source of potential theatre. Video and sound recorders become valuable aids to documenting.

Ethical issues and matters of confidentiality invariably arise here – and these are different in each context. You and the class must ensure (sometimes in writing) that respondents are willing to have their lives examined and their opinions and stories used and changed in the play. It is sometimes necessary for the students to explain that all data will be fictionalised to be individually unrecognisable. In the school TIE project described, three schools were targeted and one-third of the key class made a visit to each (transport had to be organised) and spoke at length to a parallel class, including getting signed permission from those respondents to use their stories.

Step 3: improvising

As soon as data and stories are gathered, perhaps in parallel with that process, the class can start improvising, creating scenes and exploring the dramatic possibilities of the material. Another reason for starting this as soon as possible is to get all the group actively involved in the context and feeling 'ownership' of the material.

The keynote here must be *respect for the community and its problems*. This does not mean that the raw material need be treated with reverence. It should be played with, fictionalised, pulled around and extended with the dual aims of:

○ illuminating and giving insights into the community context
○ making the stories and material theatrically interesting.

A wide range of improvisational techniques can be used. 'Headlines' playbuilding and some of the techniques incorporated within are valuable starters. Process drama techniques are also useful.

To prevent disappointment later, it is important early to stress that many improvisations will happen and much of the material generated will not find its way into the final product, though it may be very good in itself. Another important point to make at the outset is that whatever characters students play in improvisations, they will not necessarily play those characters if they are written into the final product (see below).

Although there will be a strong impetus to create scenes to be performed, this should not drive the process. For instance, if a story is interesting and thought-provoking, to explore it further by 'hot-seating' some of the characters, or creating a time-jump to explore the background of latent conflict or the consequences of a stalemate . . . all of these techniques will immediately give interesting new lines to pursue and also start to flesh out those characters in case any of them are retained in the final performance. It needs to be remembered also that the audience is to be integrally involved in some way (see below).

Some of the scenes should definitely be role-played seriously, to help the students find empathy and discover the authenticity of the situations (after all, they are dealing with real life local issues).

It is usually wise not to seize on the exact shape or defining style of the play too early. This often closes the door on better ideas. However, a basic structural idea will probably emerge quite quickly – say a single story to be dramatised, or a collage of stories to be woven together.

Step 4: refining and scripting

During this period students should be aware that a lot of the material that they generate in the improvisations will not be able to be used but they should be encouraged to document those scenes or moments that seem significant or likely to be usable. They may be encouraged to tape-record dialogue or even write fragments of script.

Other forms of writing will also prove very valuable, often more so than the first tentative written dialogue. Ask the students to do some in-role writing, that is, as a character, writing or speaking in the first person: a diary entry for instance, or an angry letter to the editor, or a talkback radio tirade. Often asking the students to write a song or poem that crystallises some aspect of the conflict will produce powerful material that may not be immediately usable but might provide a powerful or moving moment in the final production.

As the ideas clarify, a structure and stylistic ideas will begin to emerge. Although the community context of bullying or conflict is very real, and so will be much of the early improvisation and role-play, it is a good idea to introduce the notion of using non-naturalistic theatrical conventions. For one thing, effective naturalistic script and acting are both very difficult. The students will be quick to notice with dissatisfaction that their first scripting or performing efforts, based on trying to recapture powerful empathic role-play, usually come out like bad television soap opera.

There is another, even more important dramatic reason for bringing in non-naturalistic elements: to find and experiment with dramatic irony. Distanced theatrical conventions re-create or refract a story in a fresh, unexpected way that creates new insight and understanding, by contrast, into the theme or the relationship.

The teacher can suggest that scenes be re-created in entirely non-naturalistic ways, for example:

- as dance or stylised movement
- re-telling the story as a fairytale
- re-creating the essence of the scene symbolically using no more than ten words
- re-creating some aspect as a comic patter act
- turning the story into a game, a new sport or a game-show
- turning the story into a ritual
- turning it into grotesque slapstick.

Several of these devices involve finding some kind of analogy for the context and the issues – myths or legends, for instance. This can often prove very valuable in providing a framework for the eventual performance, for another reason: the community context of bullying and conflict by its very nature will involve sensitivities and potentially high emotions. If the performance is to create thought and entertainment, rather than pain and anger, those sensitivities need to be distanced. Some kind of distance and irony are essential to provide the audience with **protection** – an emotional safety net – so that they can recognise the relevance of the piece but not feel personally threatened.

As the students become more confident and skilled with the improvisational process, another useful way of developing the material is to ask the students either to revisit scenes and situations, or to develop new ones. They must include at least one or two non-naturalistic or symbolic elements in the scene so that it is still recognisable as a scene that tells a story, but sharpened up and made more arresting. Sometimes it is valuable to prescribe these as a compulsory constraint and here are a few useful techniques:

- a soliloquy – a character stepping out and addressing the audience directly
- percussion instruments (supply a few), so that key moments are underlined in sound
- masks for at least one character throughout
- a song or the chorus of a song included more than once
- at the climax, an 'alienating' moment of slapstick or grotesquerie.

The class should aim to provide 20–30 minutes of quality performance – more than that is not usually reasonable. The whole performance will be extended by the use of audience participation, as appropriate to the particular audience and context. The extent to which the teacher needs to shape and even write the final script will vary, according to the age and skills level of the class and the difficulty of the community context.

Step 5: considering the audience

It is necessary during the above steps for the students to relate to and explore the context and material in their own terms – though the community's perspectives will impact on this. Before the final shaping of the piece the audience must be reconsidered – their interests, concerns and needs must become the centre of the process.

Firstly, the play must excite and entertain the audience, even though the subject matter may be close and painful. The class must consider next what they want their performance to achieve, in terms of the issue at stake. The play must *not* attempt to offer solutions, preach or tell the audience 'what they ought to know' – to make any didactic statement. It is important to stress that offering solutions to other people's problems is arrogant and trivialises the issues – and after all, not all conflicts can be resolved.

In some way the play should open up the subject in a way that the audience will respond to and recognise as relevant, but not find intrusive, accusatory or threatening. Within these constraints it should seek to be provocative and raise rather than seek to answer questions. In conflict handling terms, the performance is like a meeting with a mediator. The mediator does not tell the protagonists what to do but tries to help them look coolly enough at the issue to reshape their reactions and thinking and allow the possibility of negotiation, and eventually help them listen to the other side.

When bullying is the central focus of the performance, it is essential not to concentrate just on the victim or the bully, or to blame individuals or the community for the problem. As with the conflict EFT in the main program, the Community TIE play should offer perspectives on the problem and possible effective approaches to handling it.

Step 6: devising audience participation

This is where the audience participation comes in. Rather than just showing them the issue or portraying their bullying experiences or conflicts for them to think about, this kind of theatre can give them a chance to address actively their concerns – protected by the fiction ('this isn't me doing this – it's only a play'). With the students leading, they can join in a community exploration and productive discussion that is designed to raise the issues in fresh ways.

Audience participation needs to be carefully set up, particularly for adults. For one thing, the idea of audience participation transgresses against people's expectation of what happens in theatre: that an audience sits and watches – usually safely in the dark – while others act.

The performers do start with a number of factors on their side in this:

○ They are young and their energy, commitment and sincerity has a great deal of appeal to most audiences.

○ They are not professionals whose very performing skills are often a barrier to an audience who feel unequal to contributing on the same platform.

○ Some of the audience are likely to already have been involved as respondents in the research stage and feel 'ownership' – that they already have a hand in the play.

○ The students are likely to be known to a proportion of the audience – at least to research respondents and other friends or relatives from within the community.

○ The issues being portrayed are close to the hearts of the audience.

It has already been demonstrated in the EFT how an audience can be encouraged to join in a performance as **spect-actors**. It is important that they are aware from the start both that they are going to be taking an active part, and that they will not be expected to do anything uncomfortable. The next thing is to beguile them into wanting to take part. By the time the spect-actors are invited into the performance, they have seen a full-on destructive conflict and it is a natural human reaction to want to join in and help resolve a conflict – especially if you like the people involved.

Forum theatre actually originated in community theatre and 'spect-acting' is one of the natural techniques that can be adapted to audience participation in theatre in education. The other mainstay comes from process drama: 'hot-seating'. This hot-seating can be at the end of the performance and lead into a critical discussion among the performers and the audience. Alternatively, it can be in the middle, where the action is frozen and the audience invited to put a character on the spot or offer advice. The crucial factor is for a question to have been posed that the audience has a stake in answering ('Whose fault was it?' 'How can we get round that problem?'). So the audience will want to talk to the character to find out more, in order to help solve that question by cross-examining the character: ('Why did you walk away?' 'Couldn't you see that would escalate the conflict?'). In some clever plays, the scene can proceed differently according to the advice, or the majority vote, of the audience.

It is quite a good idea to have a few students in the audience as 'plants' primed and ready to ask a question in the hot-seat or make a spect-actor **intervention**. This is as much for the sake of allaying the students' anxieties as for the need to fill an embarrassed vacuum. If plants are used, it must be made clear to them not to hog the limelight and to give the real audience time to gather their wits and contribute.

If the audience is small and willing, some of the other techniques of process drama might be invoked as audience participation: such as asking them to do a role-play, or play a game, or engage in some piece of dramatic reconstruction. The limits of the participation are defined by the space, the time, the actors' levels of skill and control and the contract that can be established with the audience. It should be remembered that students are not teachers or professional group managers and for some staying in role without a script (as is necessary in hot-seating) is quite difficult.

Period 2: production

Step 7: casting

Decisions about casting the performance should be left until the beginning of rehearsals. Even if – as will certainly happen – individuals have played a particular character through one or more improvisations, it should not be seen to be their prerogative (or burden) to play that character in the final play. Although it may be tempting to an experienced drama teacher to cast the play, our experience suggests that in a group-devised piece it can usually best be left to the students. This way they keep ownership of the piece, whereas teacher's decisions can cause rifts and disappointment. The teacher usually will need to control the process and a lesson or at least half an hour should be devoted to it. This in itself is a very useful learning experience and revealing to the teacher.

Step 8: let the rehearsals begin!

The rehearsals then proceed as normal for any production, but with two additional elements:

○ The particular audience needs to be kept constantly in mind. It can be healthy and helpful to invite one of the original respondents, or one of the community's leaders, to a rehearsal, to check a scene's authenticity, or give advice (and this invariably has the spin-off benefit of increasing anticipation in the audience!).
○ The audience participation has to be prepared for and practised. This is not easy to do as there is no script to rehearse.

Particularly for techniques like hot-seating the actors must work hard in **backgrounding** their characters. The participation element will fall flat and the whole effect of the play will be lost if the characters cannot effectively and consistently sustain their roles. Student actors are normally much more fearless in this task than professional actors – who may be lost without their scripts – but they can be cavalier or not realise the importance of deep backgrounding.

Then, both for hot-seating and forum theatre, dummy-runs must be practised where all the likely questions are asked and fielded and the possible interventions are considered and tried out.

Period 3: performance

If Periods 1 and 2 have been effectively managed, then the performance will take care of itself. As is well known in theatre, it's usually all right on the night and students invariably surprise their teachers by rising to unexpected heights when confronted by the moment of truth on stage. The students are young and full of good faith because they are bravely presenting matters of real concern to the audience. The audience feels privileged to have been singled out and respected, and intrigued to find out what the youngsters have made of it all.

Using some method to gauge and analyse audience response is often a good idea as a strong reinforcer of the learning . . . or even a corrector of the performers' misapprehensions! If time permits, a visit to the community or the initial respondents following the performance is very valuable. The community and the students can reflect together and discuss how they addressed the issues and whether they made a realistic or substantive contribution.

Something of this intention will in fact happen informally if the actors and audience are encouraged to mingle informally and talk after the performance. The audience will be polite, but individual useful points of response can be garnered and pooled by the class in reflective discussion on another occasion.

Giving out a questionnaire to the audience can be useful for the class's reflective discussion, though again this is, for the audience, something of an anti-climax.

Whatever happens with the audience itself it is crucial that sufficient time is allowed for a thorough reflective discussion, far enough from the performance for the group to have come down to earth and be able to be a little dispassionate. This discussion should be as soon as possible brought round to bear on the substantive community conflict issues that initiated the project and the class should consider three themes:

○ what effect the performance may have had, or might reasonably be expected to have
○ what the class themselves have learned about that arena of conflict and about their own community

○ what the project has taught them or reinforced for them about the nature of bullying or conflict: about interests, rights and power, about the assumptions and stereotypes that underlie conflict, about the roles of the bully, bullied and bystander, and about how bullying and conflict escalate in the community and what measures individuals and groups can take to de-escalate them.

Any one of these themes, or all of them, can form the basis of a very significant assignment to assess not only what the students have learnt through their contact with Community TIE but also what they now *know* they know.

glossary of specialised terms

This glossary of terms is not intended to be comprehensive in regard to either conflict theory or drama, both of which have extensive and sometimes contested specialised terminologies. The terms found here are only those that appear in the pages of this book, and they are defined only in the way in which they are used here.

Terms within the definitions in **bold** font are also defined elsewhere in the glossary.

Cooling conflict program terminology

(All these terms are explained in detail in Chapter 4.)

Coordinator The teacher or teacher–administrator, preferably at Deputy Principal level, who is responsible for initiating, supporting and maintaining *Cooling Conflict*.

In-service *Cooling Conflict* is normally preceded by an in-service professional development program for at least the **Coordinator**, **Key teachers** and **Relay teachers**, and preferably other teachers and school administrators. This may entail specialised training days, in-class supervision, and informal mentoring.

Key class The class in a school where *Cooling Conflict* begins, and where the students are given the most detailed experiences of learning about conflict through drama, in order for them to start the rounds of peer teaching. This is normally a senior secondary school Drama class.

Key teacher The teacher of the **Key class**, who starts the program and often oversees the use of drama in the program throughout the school. This is preferably a senior Drama teacher, and normally a teacher with some training and experience in drama education is necessary.

Management committee A committee of stakeholders set up in a school or school cluster implementing *Cooling Conflict*, in order to oversee and facilitate the implementation of the program.

Relay classes The **first relay classes** are the classes of students younger than the **Key class** who receive the first peer teaching, from the Key class. These are normally and preferably not Drama classes.

The **second relay classes** are the classes of younger students, normally in the primary school, who receive the second round of peer teaching from the **first relay class**.

The **third** and **fourth relay classes** are classes of progressively younger children who receive peer teaching from their elders, and if available pass the knowledge on to even younger students.

Relay teachers The teachers of the **Relay classes** who supervise the peer teaching of their own classes by older students, and assist their classes to prepare for peer teaching students more junior. They are normally not Drama teachers, and will tie the *Cooling Conflict* program into their normal curriculum work.

Conflict and bullying terminology

(The nature of bullying and conflict and the terminology associated with them are dealt with in detail in Chapter 1.)

Accommodation A response to conflict or bullying whereby a **protagonist** seeks to de-escalate or resolve the conflict by yielding to the pressure and giving in.

Aggression A state of behaviour in a conflict situation, or a response to it, whereby a **protagonist** attempts to assert power over their **antagonist**, often with violence.

Antagonist A party directly involved in a conflict, as defined from the point of view of the other main party, the **protagonist**.

Assertion A response to conflict or bullying where a **protagonist** acknowledges the conflict or bullying and seeks to address it by direct and assertive action. This is often known as **confronting** or fronting the issue.

Avoidance A response to bullying and conflict whereby a **protagonist** seeks to avoid situations or contexts where the conflict can be made **manifest** or **escalated**.

Brewing conflict See **Emerging conflict**.

Bullied People who are being oppressed or otherwise suffer the systematic misuse of power in a particular context.

Bully, bullies People who misuse power to systematically oppress those less powerful in a particular context.

Bullying Repeated oppression, psychological or physical, of a less powerful person by a more powerful person or group of persons.

Bystanders People who permit or encourage bullying in a particular context and are therefore complicit in it.

Conflict An opposition of ideas, interests or actions that results in a struggle over rights, status, power or resources. Conflict acknowledges or makes explicit the tensions between competing forces.

Confrontation A moment, meeting or incident where conflict is made **manifest**.

Confronting or fronting See **Assertion**.

De-escalation The lessening of destructive tension in a conflict.

Emerging conflict or bullying The second phase of conflict, where the conditions for conflict or bullying are forming themselves into a clash. In this phase, some of those affected are dimly or partially aware of the nature of the situation. Early in the research project, this phase was called *brewing*.

Escalation, escalate In any bullying situation or conflict, there is the potential for the situation to become progressively more serious (escalate) and its manifestations more apparent and sustained. When this occurs, the bullying or conflict is described as escalating.

Interests The goals or objects that people want, demand or claim. They include the underlying motivations and can be substantive, psychological or procedural.

Latent conflict or bullying The first phase of conflict where the conditions for conflict exist – a potential tension of interests, rights or power, which has not yet reached the stage of a clash. This is characterised by some or all of those affected being quite unaware of any problem.

Manifest conflict or bullying The third phase of conflict, when the conflict is resulting in action that is visible and unmistakable to all, usually with anger, frustration and often violence.

Mediation   The use of a third party, usually from outside a conflict situation, to attempt to de-escalate or resolve the conflict by negotiation.

Misunderstandings   These occur when the parties in a conflict believe or perceive that the issues between them are real and substantive when in fact they are based on prejudice, stereotyping or misinformation. Misunderstandings inevitably invoke the perception that a **right**, **interest** or **power** position is at stake.

Phases of conflict and bullying   Conflicts and bullying tend to **escalate** in three quite clearly identifiable phases: **latent**, **emerging** and **manifest**.

Power   A state of authority, status, influence or control over finance, resources or relationships.

Protagonist   One of the central figures involved in a conflict. To each protagonist, the person or persons with whom they are in conflict arc their **antagonists**.

Resolution   A state whereby the clashes of **interests**, **rights** and **power**, together with **misunderstandings** that led to a conflict or bullying situation, no longer exist and animosity has been dispelled.

Rights   The standards or values that define what is fair and appropriate or determines what parties are entitled to.

Stereotyping   Ascribing to another person certain exaggerated and typical characteristics regarding their attitudes and behaviour which are based not on a knowledge of the person involved, but on prejudices based on factors such as their culture, ethnic origin, gender, ideology or age.

Drama terminology

(These terms are dealt with in more detail in Chapters 6 and 7.)

Backgrounding   Exercises or techniques used to assist actors or participants in **role-play** to establish more fictional history about the **characters**, or flesh out the **characterisation**.

Boal, Augusto   Brazilian theatre educator and founder of **Theatre of the Oppressed** and other theatrical movements designed to give real-life empowerment to communities through active participation in forms of participatory theatre.

Bolton, Gavin   British pioneer of **drama in education** with **Dorothy Heathcote**. These two were instrumental in forging a new pedagogy based on **experiential role-play** and other improvised drama and theatre forms.

Character, characterisation   A fictional person depicted in a play or other form of drama. **Characterisation** is the process of fleshing out the details of the person until it is realistic, multi-faceted and believable.

Community theatre in education   See **Theatre in education**.

Confessions   A sequence of storytelling labelled by the authors for generating and fictionalising stories of conflict and bullying from real life by drama participants for use in **enhanced forum theatre**.

Distance   This refers in drama to the emotional distance between an actor or audience member and the dramatic action or character that is necessary in order to reflect on the action or character dispassionately or critically. It is the obverse of **empathy**.

Drama in education   The use of mainly improvised drama structures for teaching purposes, often in curricular areas other than Drama, and usually embracing contemporary social issues and problems. The main form used is **process drama**.

EFT   See **Enhanced forum theatre**.

Empathy   A basic requirement of any act of drama or theatre: the ability of a participant, whether actor or audience, to 'step into another's shoes' and identify at least to a degree emotionally and intellectually with that person. It is the obverse of **distance**.

Enhanced forum theatre (EFT)   This is the central drama strategy of *Cooling Conflict*. It comprises a sequence of performance activities involving audience participation, based on **Forum theatre** and enhanced by **process drama**.

Enrolment   When preparing participants for **role-play** it is often necessary to use exercises and activities to help them build belief in their roles. This is enrolment.

Experiential role-play   See **role-play**.

Forum theatre   A performance of a problem-based scene or scenes, where the audience are invited to intervene as **spect-actors** to resolve the problem. The technique was originally devised for **Theatre of the Oppressed**.

Freeze This is the conventional term in participatory theatre and drama for stopping the play, in order to comment on or change the dramatic action while the actors remain immobile.

Freeze-frames Sometimes known as 'tableaux' or 'still images', actors are arranged in a posture representing a particular moment in a play or improvised drama, and remain immobile for observation or reflection by an audience.

Headlines A sequence of dramatic techniques labelled by the authors for generating true-to-life fictional conflicts and bullying episodes with drama participants.

Heathcote, Dorothy British pioneer of **drama in education** with **Gavin Bolton**. These two were instrumental in forging a new pedagogy based on **experiential role-play** and other improvised drama and theatre forms.

Host In an **enhanced forum theatre** presentation, the **host** acts as the compère or master of ceremonies, introducing the play and setting the scene, then controlling the audience participation and **interventions**.

Hot-seat and hot-seating A technique from **process drama** that involves audience members or fellow-participants in close questioning of another player, seated in role as a **character** in a play or emerging drama, in order to find or establish the character's history or deeper motivations.

Interventions In **forum theatre** and **enhanced forum theatre** members of the audience are invited to freeze the action and step into the play in the role of one of the actors.

Joker This is the name originally used in **forum theatre** for the figure called in this book the **host**.

Magic In forum theatre, a **spect-actor's intervention** may be challenged by other audience members as 'Magic!' if they believe that it is either improbable and far-fetched, or untrue to the nature and likely behaviour of the character.

Multiple role, multiple role circle A theatrical and rehearsal convention, often used in devising or **backgrounding** a new piece of drama, where a number of actors simultaneously take on the role of a **character** in the story, for questioning. **Multiple role circle**, one manifestation of this technique, is intended to generate quickly fictional but believable stories of conflict or bullying for use in **enhanced forum theatre**.

Playbuilding A range of methods of devising a play for performance by a group of participants using forms of dramatic improvisation and other collaborative practical activities. This may be led by a teacher or playwright, but the material is mainly generated by the group.

Procedural role-play See **role-play**.

Process drama An improvised drama form for active participants with no formal performance or external audience. It comprises structured **role-play** techniques including **experiential role-play** combined with other theatrical conventions and rehearsal exercises. It usually forms a significant part of **drama in education** and the terms are sometimes interchangeable.

Protection Dramatic techniques of fictionalising and **distancing** the action in drama, in order to shield the participants from potential discomfort or from real-life consequences of the disclosure of personal stories or details about conflict and bullying.

Relaxation An important quality to achieve some intentions in **process drama** or acting. There are countless methods of relaxation; one simple method is described in Chapter 7.

Role circle A technique of process drama for developing the dramatic action or storyline, where the group stands in a circle. Each takes on the role of somebody connected with the emerging story; each offers one invented piece of relevant and new 'information'.

Role-play This is where participants are asked to identify with someone other than themselves, and enact a situation involving that person in order to explore or depict that person's behaviour. This may involve an audience, in order to depict that person's expected or desired behaviour, or it may be just for the purposes of exploring the behaviour. In **procedural role-play** players are given tightly defined behavioural procedures to follow, and they may follow a script. In **experiential role-play** players are asked to identify or empathise with the person and behave naturally as that person, or as they would in that situation; this often entails **enrolment** exercises.

Scene Four In **enhanced forum theatre**, an extension of the original play, devised or suggested by the audience, endeavouring to resolve the conflict or bullying through mediation at another time and place from the scenes depicted.

Spect-actor A term invented by **Augusto Boal** to define the role of audience members who are invited to take an active role in a piece of theatre, such as **intervention** in **forum theatre**.

Theatre for development (TFD)   A movement in theatre in developing countries over the last 30 years, using theatre and drama as methods of encouraging a range of social outcomes, including social development, education and health education, political awareness, communication in rural areas with little access to literacy or mass media, and community self-esteem and expression. Described further in Chapter 2.

Theatre in education (TIE)   A form of theatrical performance usually in schools by a company of actors from outside, with a primarily educational intention beyond teaching about theatre. It often incorporates some form of audience participation, workshop or discussion. **Community theatre in education** involves the company preparing a piece of theatre in education for a particular community group beyond the school.

Theatre of the oppressed (TO)   A movement in theatre originated by **Augusto Boal** with the aim of using theatre to help empower oppressed and particularly poor people to identify and counter their oppression. A central strategy of TO is **forum theatre**. Described further in Chapter 2.

Thought-tracking   A technique from **process drama** where the audience or leader can **freeze** the action to hear from one or more of the characters in the scene exactly what is going through their mind at that moment.

Visualisation   A range of warm-up exercises designed to focus students' minds and imaginations to put them in an appropriately creative frame of mind for **process drama** work. One simple version is described in Chapter 7.

Warm-up   Usually an activity or set of activities or games whose purpose is to make the students ready to take part in drama or theatre work. A warm-up may involve physical exercises to warm up body or voice, mental exercises to focus the mind or group games to create an appropriate group dynamic and energy level – in some school situations, 'warm-up' may involve cooling down exercises if the students arrive from physically active or emotionally stressful prior activities. Many examples are found in Chapter 7.

Peer teaching terminology

Peer mediation   A program whereby chosen individuals are trained in simple conflict management techniques and are then given the responsibility and authority to advise and negotiate with fellow students who are involved in a conflict or bullying situation with the aim of de-escalating it.

Peer tutoring   Where individual students assist other individuals or small groups of fellow students their own age or younger to learn specific skills or subject matter. Peer tutoring occurs most commonly in schools when students assist and listen to other students practise reading and numeracy, and in individual and small-group coaching of sporting skills.

Peer teaching   Involves individuals and small groups of students in teaching significant curriculum components in a particular subject area to groups or whole classes of younger students.

resources
for schools

1. Timeline for implementation of *Cooling Conflict*

Schools may implement *Cooling Conflict* in a number of ways, within the basic constraints laid out in Chapters 4 and 5. The chart below demonstrates how it might operate from senior secondary to junior primary school within the one four-term academic year, and indicates some of the major responsibilities for the coordinator and teachers.

Dates	Coordinator	Key teacher	Relay teachers
The previous year	Read *Cooling Conflict*, identify key class and establish support of key teacher.	Read *Cooling Conflict* and plan implementation in Drama curriculum for Term 1. Consider possible implementation and timing of Phase 4. If possible inform students.	
Before or during the first part of Term 1	Identify first relay classes. Work out Phase 1–3 timeline. Identify primary school(s) and seek support. Form management committee. Introduce program to staff meeting.	Inform students. With coordinator: work out Phase 1–3 timeline Meet with first relay class teachers. Form management committee. Introduce program to staff meeting early in Term 1.	(First relay teachers): Commit to the program. Plan appropriate curricular integration of *Cooling Conflict*.
Term 1, weeks 1–4		Teach key class through drama about conflict and introduce EFT.	

Dates	Coordinator	Key teacher	Relay teachers
Term 1, week 5		Key class meet first relay class, administer questionnaire.	First relay class meet key class, fill in questionnaire.
Term 1, weeks 6–7	In-service first and primary relay teachers (with key teacher). Preliminary arrangements for first and second relay peer teaching.	Key class sub-groups process questionnaires, construct EFT & plan for peer teaching. In-service relay teachers (with coordinator).	First and primary relay teachers attend in-service. Introductory work in curriculum unit preparing for peer teaching.
Term 1, weeks 8–9		Key class sub-groups peer teach first relay classes.	First relay classes taught by key class sub-groups.
Term 2, weeks 1–3	Detailed arrangements for first and second relay peer teaching.	If possible, key groups mentor first relay classes.	First relay classes sub-groups construct EFT & plan for peer teaching. Meet and possibly administer and process questionnaire to second relay classes.
Term 2, week 4			First relay classes sub-groups teach second relay classes.
Term 2, weeks 5–9	Management committee meeting to review progress.	Attend management committee.	Second relay classes sub-groups construct EFT and plan for peer teaching. Meet third relay classes. If appropriate, attend management committee.
Term 3	[If Phase 4 to be undertaken] Assist key teacher with community liaison and negotiation for TIE.	[If Phase 4 to be undertaken] With coordinator, start preparing key class for community TIE. Audience identified and research undertaken.	Second relay classes sub-groups peer teach third relay classes. Third relay classes construct EFT and plan for peer teaching. Meet fourth relay classes. Third relay classes sub-groups peer teach fourth relay classes.
Term 4	Management committee meeting to review *Cooling Conflict*. Preliminary planning for next year.	Rehearsal and production of TIE. Performance of TIE and reflection. Attend management committee.	Delayed relay class drama and peer teaching. Reflection on program. If appropriate, attend management committee.

2. Explanatory hand-out for key class

TO THE KEY CLASS

Drama can be especially effective in changing the way we think and behave. By taking on roles and stepping into imaginary situations we can explore what people think and do in all aspects of their lives. By doing this we increase our understanding of human behaviour and develop empathy for the feelings and experiences of others.

The *Cooling Conflict* bullying and conflict management program uses this particular power of drama to help students in schools to understand the nature and causes of conflict and to manage their own conflicts more effectively.

As senior students, you have a key part to play in making the *Cooling Conflict* program work in your school, which is why your class is called the **key class**. The program begins with you. In your normal classes you will learn about the three stages of conflict. You will use drama to explore a range of bullying and conflict situations and develop an understanding of how they escalate from stage to stage. As you become more confident in your use of bullying and conflict management you will also be learning effective strategies for exploring and managing bullying and conflict, in particular 'enhanced forum theatre'.

The next and most important job the key class has to perform is to teach younger students in the school about conflict management. This is done by your key class breaking up into groups of four to eight and each group taking responsibility for a junior class, known as the **relay class**. These relay classes will not normally be drama classes, but will be doing the *Cooling Conflict* work as part of other subjects. Just as your key class learned about conflict management through drama, you will now work in groups to teach the relay class the three stages of conflict and the use of just one drama strategy – enhanced forum theatre – to investigate their own choice of conflicts.

Each relay class will then teach other students in turn, either at their own school or at primary schools in the area. Ideally, you as peer teachers may have the opportunity of helping the relay class prepare their teaching.

Most senior students are concerned at first about having to teach other students. In fact, every time *Cooling Conflict* has been trialled in a school, this **peer teaching** has been the most successful part of the program. Younger students really enjoy being taught by their older peers, learn very effectively and behave extremely well. The senior students enjoy the experience of peer teaching, and find that teaching conflict management assists them to understand it properly, and even helps them to manage conflicts in their own lives effectively.

Cooling Conflict: A new approach to managing bullying and conflict in schools © John O'Toole, Bruce Burton and Anna Plunkett 2005 c/o Pearson Education Australia. This page may be photocopied for classroom use.

The last phase of *Cooling Conflict* involves preparing a play about conflict, which helps teach audiences about bullying and conflict management. This form of teaching theatre is called **'theatre in education'** and in Phase Four of *Cooling Conflict* you may have the chance to be involved in the preparation and performance of a theatre in education play for a community audience, which could achieve even wider benefits in your local community.

At times when you are working on this conflict management program you will find it challenging and even stressful. It is worth remembering that every senior student who has been involved in *Cooling Conflict* so far has really enjoyed it and felt it was a valuable experience. For many, it has been the highlight of their time at school.

3. Student instructions for enhanced forum theatre

TO STUDENTS

ENHANCED FORUM THEATRE CHECKLIST

In planning your enhanced forum theatre play remember that the conflicts that are worth exploring are long-term ones, not just sudden arguments. The conflict does not just escalate through the three stages in a few minutes. The deep causes always lie in attitudes and assumptions that go right back and it often takes a long time for the conflict to brew up. When you are backgrounding your forum theatre you need to think of all three stages as taking place at quite different times. At the very least there should be one day between scenes. You will find that you explore conflicts better if you make it longer – say a month, or even a year between stages.

You can plan your enhanced forum theatre play in one of two ways:

Type A: as a fictional conflict devised to be as authentic as possible and very thoroughly backgrounded and then developed into the three scenes demonstrating the three stages of conflict – **latent**, **emerging** and **manifest**.

Type B: as a reconstruction of a piece of conflict from the real life of a member of your group but fictionalised into a play that has three scenes demonstrating the three stages of conflict – **latent**, **emerging** and **manifest**.

You need to:

☐ background it thoroughly so that you are really familiar with the characters and their motives – everything that got them involved in this conflict

☐ script and block it clearly so that the audience will know enough about the situation to understand how the conflict has come about and be able to see and hear exactly what is going on in each scene

☐ rehearse it carefully so that you can repeat it exactly a number of times – it will be played at least three times in full.

You must also decide who in your group will not be in the play but will act as the **host**.

Before you perform, the host must explain to your audience:

☐ that they will be watching a conflict being portrayed and then they will be invited to join in actively to help resolve it

☐ that they will watch the first performance without comment and should watch carefully. (If the play and conflict are complicated, you may want to ask them to watch the performance twice through without comment.)

After the first performance the host will invite the audience to suggest how the conflict might have been helped by one of the characters acting differently and identify exactly at what point this might happen. At this point the host will invite the audience to suggest a character or two that they would like to **hot-seat**, in order to find out more about the character. After this, the host will introduce the second performance, explaining that the audience can stop the action at any time to **thought-track** any or all the characters. The host controls this and sets it up with the players. The host should be quite firm and set all of this up very clearly.

Following the second performance, the host will invite the audience to stop the action at any point they think something could be done to **de-escalate** the conflict. The performers will then start the third performance, with members of the audience stopping the action at any point. The host will invite the audience member, or '**spect-actor**', to come on stage and replace one of the actors in their role and try to resolve or de-escalate the conflict. (If the audience is very timid, it may be necessary in the first place for the actor him/herself to take up the suggestion and try it out in the scene, but this is a last resort.)

At this point, the host will also explain **magic!** and invite the audience to stop the revised scene if they believe magic is occurring. Then the group re-starts the scene from the freeze point, with the spect-actor trying out whatever change of behaviour they have thought of. The other actors will react in character. The group should make it as difficult as possible (just possible) for the new strategy to work. If 'magic!' is called and the audience – or just the host – agrees, the scene is stopped, the spect-actor will rejoin the audience, and another suggestion is invited.

In this third performance too, members of the audience can stop the action to request more hot-seating or thought-tracking, which the host can set up if appropriate.

You will have devised a really difficult conflict – and therefore a very good piece of enhanced forum theatre – if none of the strategies the audience tries works completely. Then you can use the next step, Scene Four.

Break the audience into sub-groups of about six. Explain that the conflict is too difficult to solve on the spot and that a mediator would talk separately to at least one of the protagonists, to cool them down and get their help in resolving the conflict.

Each group should:

☐ identify one person who might be able to mediate. It might be somebody already seen or mentioned in the scenario, or a teacher or counsellor.

☐ nominate a time and place for the meeting (that fits in with the scenario).

☐ nominate one member from the group to take on the role of that mediator.

☐ discuss and decide the strategy for addressing the conflict.

When you have given them time to decide these, ask each group in turn to explain their proposal. Then in turn, ask each group to set up the space for the mediation meeting, and nominate the characters they think would take part. Then, with one spect-actor from the group acting as the mediator, act out the meeting, with the actors making it very hard for the spect-actor to mediate.

Afterwards, discuss with the audience which of the mediation meetings would be a good idea, which would be doomed and why.

4. Specimen palm cards

Many students (and some teachers) find palm cards useful when they are publicly presenting information, particularly if they have only recently encountered it. These can be photocopied on to card, cut up and used in the peer teaching.

Conflict palm cards

Causes of conflict

Conflict is caused by a clash of *rights*, or *interests*, or *power*.

Conflict can also be caused by *misunderstanding* or by ignorance about what people are really like that leads to *stereotyping* them and not treating them like people.

Latent conflict

Latent (hidden) *conflict* is a situation ripe for conflict, where there is a clash of rights, interest or power, or a misunderstanding or negative attitude, that has not yet led to trouble – like dry bush waiting for a spark to set it ablaze.

Emerging conflict

Emerging (brewing) *conflict* is where a situation has led to the beginnings of trouble, but only some of those involved are aware of it. A spark has lit the brushwood, but there are no flames yet and only a few people can see the smoke.

Manifest conflict

Manifest (open) *conflict* is a situation where all those involved are locked in a struggle, verbal, physical or emotional, and the conflict is there for all to see. The bush is ablaze.

Enhanced forum theatre palm cards

Enhanced forum theatre

This is a play designed to allow the audience to stop the action at any time and step into the play as one of the characters, to try and change the situation or resolve the conflict. The original play ends with a freeze at the key moment of manifest conflict.

Three scenes

The forum theatre play should have three separate scenes, each showing one stage of the conflict – **latent**, **emerging** and **manifest**. Remember that conflicts take time to develop so there should be considerable time gaps between each scene.

Intervention

Any member of the audience can intervene by asking the host to stop the play. They then take the place of any one of the characters and try to manage the conflict. The audience member can also ask the host to rewind the action to the place where they want to intervene.

The host

Like a game show compère, the host introduces and controls the play. He or she explains forum theatre to the audience, tells the actors to run the play a number of times and then invites the audience to step in next time it runs. The host also makes the final decision as to whether magic has been used.

Magic

This is where an improbable or unbelievable resolution to the conflict is tried. Magic happens when an audience member takes on a role in the play and says or does something unlikely or impossible to end the conflict, such as winning Gold Lotto or suddenly treating an enemy as a friend for no reason. The host or the audience calls 'magic' and the play begins again at the point just before the magic was introduced.

5. Specimen student questionnaire

This can be administered by at least the key and first relay classes to their intending peer learners, to help identify the concerns and attitudes of the younger students towards conflict and bullying, and the kinds of conflict that they encounter. Alternatively it may be of use to teachers, such as the key class teacher, to administer, for the same reason.

The questionnaire has been focused on **conflict** rather than **bullying** because the word 'conflict' is both more generic and more value-neutral than 'bullying'. Instances of bullying behaviour will certainly be thrown up by it, among other kinds of conflict. It would be easy to re-design this questionnaire to focus more specifically on bullying, if this is the emphasis that the *Cooling Conflict* team wish it to have.

SPECIMEN STUDENT QUESTIONNAIRE

QUESTION A

A1   Are you
   1.   Male   ☐
   2.   Female   ☐

A2.   Were you *and* your parents
   1.   All born in Australia   ☐
   2.   Not all born in Australia   ☐

A3.   Are you from
   1.   A mainly British- or Irish-Australian background   ☐
   2.   Another background   ☐
           Explain, if you like: _____

QUESTION B

Think of the word *conflict* – and think of an example. Where is, or was, the first conflict that comes into your mind?
   1.   at school   ☐
   2.   in your family   ☐
   3.   in somebody else's family   ☐
   4.   in your local community   ☐
   5.   an international conflict   ☐
   6.   a fictional conflict on TV or in a book   ☐

QUESTION C

Which type of person are you?
   1.   One who tries to avoid conflicts at all cost   ☐
   2.   One who doesn't look for conflicts but doesn't avoid them   ☐
   3.   One who sometimes likes to be involved in conflict   ☐

QUESTION D

What do you think is the major cause of conflicts happening at school since you have been there? Rank these in order (put the Number 1 in the box you think is *the* major cause, and 7 as least true):

1.   rivalries between groups ☐

2.   personal feuds ☐

3.   bullying ☐

4.   conflict between teachers and students ☐

5.   conflicts between girls and boys ☐

6.   some other cause ☐

7.   no serious conflicts ☐

QUESTION E

E1.   Have you been personally involved in any serious conflicts at school *in the last twelve months* as a protagonist (one of the people in the conflict)?

    1.   Yes ☐

    2.   No ☐

E2.   If 'yes', who was the conflict mainly between?

    1.   you and another individual student ☐

    2.   your group of students and another group ☐

    3.   you individually and another group ☐

    4.   you and a teacher ☐

    5.   you and somebody else – an outsider or parent ☐

    6.   more than two people or groups ☐

E3.   What stage is the conflict in now?

    1.   fully resolved (sorted out to everyone's satisfaction) ☐

Cooling Conflict: A new approach to managing bullying and conflict in schools © John O'Toole, Bruce Burton and Anna Plunkett 2005 c/o Pearson Education Australia. This page may be photocopied for classroom use.

2.   partly resolved ☐

3.   unresolved ☐

QUESTION F

Think of one conflict at school that you were *not* involved in personally, but as a friend or an interested bystander.

F1.   Did you take sides in the conflict?

    1.   Yes ☐

    2.   No ☐

F2.   Did you try to intervene (join in to sort it out)?

    1.   Yes ☐

    2.   No ☐

F3.   Was the conflict resolved?

    1.   Yes ☐

    2.   No ☐

QUESTION G

G1.   Do you think boys or girls get into conflict more?

    1.   Boys ☐

    2.   Girls ☐

    3.   Neither ☐

G2. What is the main kind of conflict boys get involved in?

_____

_____

G3. What is the main kind of conflict that girls get involved in?

_____

_____

G4. What is the main cause of conflict between boys and girls?

_____

_____

QUESTION H

If it was announced that for the third year running, the school captain was to be a Chinese student, how would you react?

1. be proud ☐
2. think it was unfair ☐
3. not care ☐

Explain, if you like:

_____

_____

QUESTION I

If you discovered a Year 9 student in tears, claiming a Year 8 student was bullying him or her, what would you do?

1. Ignore it ☐
2. Talk to the bully to try to get him or her to stop ☐
3. Stand over the bully to see how he or she liked it ☐
4. Tell the victim to toughen up and not be a wimp ☐

5. Try to bring the two together to discuss the problem ☐

6. Do something else – what? _____

Why? _____
_____

QUESTION J

J1. If you were suddenly to find out (however far-fetched it may seem) that your great grand-father was Aboriginal, how would you react?

1. I would be pleased ☐
2. I would be sorry ☐
3. I would not care ☐
4. . I would have a different or mixed reaction ☐

Explain, if you like:

_____
_____

J2. Would you tell people at school?

1. Yes ☐
2. No ☐

Explain, if you like:

_____
_____

6. Diagram of room setting for enhanced forum theatre

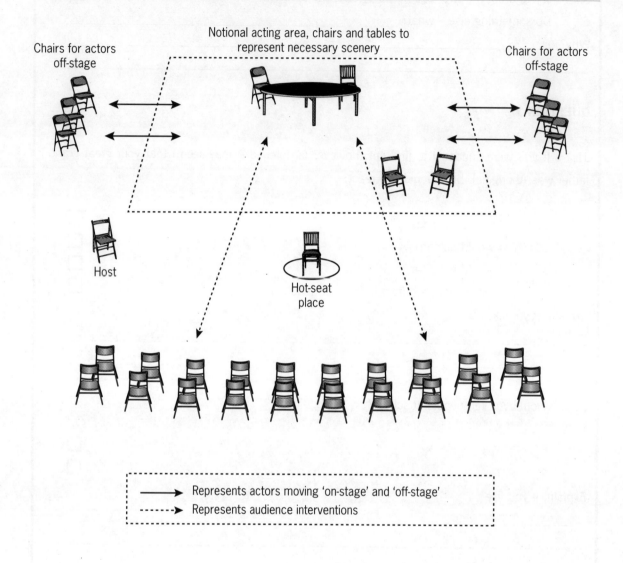

bibliography

These are some of the books and other resources that have helped to inform *Cooling Conflict*. They are all resources that should be fairly readily available through libraries, journals, websites or the publishers. The authors of this book do not agree with all of them, and many of them do not agree with each other. However, any or all of them are worth investigating for those readers who want to know more about the theory, practice and background of conflict and bullying, drama education, or peer teaching.

1. Conflict and bullying

Adler, P. & Adler, P. (1996) Preadolescent Clique Stratification and the Hierarchy of Identity. *Sociological Inquiry*, vol. 66, no. 2.

Alternative Dispute Resolution Branch (1999) *Conciliation Skills Training*. Brisbane: Department of Justice and Attorney-General.

Arrington, E. (1987) Managing Children's Conflict: A Challenge for the School Counselor. *The School Counselor*, vol. 3, pp. 188–194.

Augsburger, D. (1992) *Conflict Mediation Across Cultures: Pathways and Patterns*. Louisville, KY: Westminster/John Knox Press.

Australian Education Authorities (2002) *Bullyingnoway* [Electronic resource: www.bullyingnoway. com.au]. Brisbane: Education Queensland.

Australian Government (1994) *Sticks and Stones: Report on Violence in Australian Schools*. Canberra: Australian Government Printing Service.

Bagshaw, D. (1998) What Adolescents Say about Conflict in Secondary Schools. *Children Australia*, 23 (3).

Bagshaw, D. & Halliday, D. (2000) Handling Conflicts at School: Drama as a Medium for Adolescent Learning. *NADIE Journal (Drama Australia Journal)*, 24 (2).

Beane, A. (2000) The Bully-Free Classroom (Effective Strategies and Activities to Stop Bullying before it Starts). *Instructor*, vol. 110.

Bouhours, T. (2003) *Exclusion & Inclusion: The Impact of Schooling on Students*. Brisbane: Griffith University.

Boulding, E. (1998) Peace Culture: The Problem of Managing Human Difference. *Cross Currents*, vol. 48, no. 4.

Carr-Gregg, M. (2000) *Conference Address: Qld Association of State School Principals*. Brisbane, April.

Coyle, S. & French, D. (1996) *The Whole School Anti-Racism Project*. Sydney: New South Wales Department of School Education.

Craig, W. & Pepler, D. (2000) Observations of Bullying and Victimization in the Schoolyard, in Wendy Craig (ed.), *Childhood Social Development: The Essential Readings*. Malden, MA: Blackwell.

Deutsch, M. (1991) Educating Beyond Hate. *Peace, Environment and Education*, 2 (4).

Elliott, M. (1981) *Bullying: A Practical Guide to Coping for Schools*. Harlow, UK: Longman.

Erikson, E. (1968) *Identity: Youth and Crisis*. New York: Norton.

Field, E. (1999) *Bully Busting*. Sydney: Finch.

Fisher, R. et al. (1991) *Getting to Yes* (2nd edn). Ringwood, Victoria: Penguin Books.

Forero, R. et al. (1999) Bullying Behaviour and Psychosocial Health among School Students in New South Wales, Australia: Cross Sectional Survey (statistical data included). *British Medical Journal*, vol. 319, no. 7206.

Freire, P. (1972) *Pedagogy of the Oppressed*. London: Penguin.

Glover, D. et al. (1998) *Towards Bully-Free Schools: Interventions in Action*. Buckingham: Open University.

Hall, J. (1987) Parent–Adolescent Conflict: An Empirical View. *Adolescence*, 12.

Hamachek, D. (2000) Dynamics of Self-Understanding and Self-Knowledge: Acquisition, Advantages, and Relation to Emotional Intelligence, in R.D. Herring (ed.), *The Journal of Humanistic Counseling, Education and Development*, 38 (4), June.

Healy, K. (ed.) (1998) *Bullying and Peer Pressure*. Sydney: The Spinney Press.

Johnson, D. (1981) *Reaching Out: Interpersonal Effectiveness and Self-Actualization* (2nd edn). Englewood Cliffs, NJ: Prentice-Hall.

Johnson, D. & Johnson, F. (1991) *Joining Together. Group Theory and Group Skills* (4th edn). Englewood Cliffs, NJ: Prentice Hall.

Johnson, D. et al. (1994) Effects of Conflict Resolution Training on Elementary School Students. *The Journal of Social Psychology*, vol. 134, no. 6.

Johnson, D. & Johnson, R. (1996) Teaching All Students How to Manage Conflicts Constructively: The Peacemakers Program. *Journal of Negro Education*, vol. 65, no. 3.

King, G. & Squire, R. (1994) *Bullying at School.* Bendigo, Victoria: Bendigo Video Education.

Laursen, B. & Koplas, A. (1995) What's Important about Important Conflicts? Adolescents' Perceptions of Daily Disagreements. *Merrill-Palmer Quarterly*, 41 (4).

Liebmann, M. (ed.) (1996) *Arts Approaches to Conflict.* Bristol, UK: Jessica Kingsley Publishers.

Linke, P. (1998) *Let's Stop Bullying.* Canberra: Early Childhood Association.

Luke, J. & Myers, C. (1994) Towards Peace: Using Literature to Aid Conflict Resolution. *Childhood Education*, vol. 71, no. 2.

McCarthy, P. et al. (eds) (2001) *Bullying: From Backyard to Boardroom.* Sydney: Millennium Books.

McClure, B.A. et al. (1992) Conflict Within a Children's Group: Suggestions for Facilitating its Expression and Resolution Strategies. *The School Counselor*, 39, March.

Masheder, M. (1998) *Freedom from Bullying.* Rendlesham: Green Print.

Mitchell, R. & Mitchell, R. (1984) Constructive Management of Conflict in Groups. *Journal for Specialists in Group Work*, 9 (3).

Munro, J. (1999) *Cross-Gender Bullying Behaviour.* Ballina, NSW: Behaviour & Learning Clinic.

Munthe, E. & Roland, E. (1989) *Bullying, an International Perspective.* London: David Fulton.

Murphy, E. & Lewers, R. (2000) *The Hidden Hurt.* Ballarat, Victoria: Wizard Books.

Office of Multicultural Affairs (1991) *National Enquiry into Racist Violence.* Canberra (Chapter 8).

Olweus, D. (1993) *Bullying at School: What We Know and What We Can Do.* Oxford, UK: Blackwell.

Opotow, S. (1991) Adolescent Peer Conflicts. Implications for Students and for Schools. *Education and Urban Society*, 23 (4), August.

Rigby, K. (1996) *Bullying in Schools – and what to do about it.* Melbourne: Australian Council for Educational Research.

Rigby, K. (2002) *A Meta-Evaluation of Methods and Approaches to Reducing Bullying in Pre-Schools and Early Primary School in Australia.* Canberra: Commonwealth Attorney-General.

Rigby, K. (2002) *Bullying: A Whole-School Approach.* Melbourne: ACER.

Rotary International (1999) *Coping with Bullying* [CD-Rom]. Ashington, UK: SMS Media.

Sanders, M. (2001) Beating Bullying. Queensland Families: Practical Information for Parents and Families (2nd edn). *Queensland Families Magazine.* Brisbane: Queensland Government.

Sherif, M. & Sherif, C. (1965) Problems of Youth in Transition, in M. Sherif & C.W. Sherif (eds), *Problems of Youth: Transition to Adulthood in a Changing World.* Chicago, IL: Aldine Publishing Company.

Shure, M. (2000) Bullies and Their Victims: A Problem-Solving Approach to Prevention. *The Brown University Child and Adolescent Behavior Letter,* vol. 16, no. 10.

Slee, P. (1997) *The P.E.A.C.E. Pack.* Adelaide: Self-published.

Sullivan, K. (2000) *The Anti-Bullying Handbook.* Auckland: OUP.

Tattum, D. & Herbert, G. (1997) *Bullying: Home, School and Community.* London: David Fulton.

Varnava, G. (2002) *How to Stop Bullying in Your School.* London: David Fulton.

Wall J. Jr & Roberts Callister, R. (1995) Conflict and its Management. (Special Issue: Yearly Review of Management) *Journal of Management,* vol. 21, no. 3.

2. Drama

Boal, A. (1979) *Theatre of the Oppressed.* London: Pluto Press.

Boal, A. (1992) *Games for Actors and Non-Actors.* London: Routledge.

Boal, A. (1995) *The Rainbow of Desire: The Boal Method of Theatre and Therapy.* London: Routledge.

Bolton, G. (1979) *Towards a Theory of Drama in Education.* London: Longman.

Bolton, G. (1984) *Drama as Education: An Argument for Placing Drama at the Centre of the Curriculum.* London: Longman Group Limited.

Bolton, G. (1995) DRAMA/Drama and Cultural Values, in P. Taylor & C. Hoepper (eds), *IDEA '95: Selected Readings in Drama and Theatre Education,* pp. 29–34. Brisbane: NADIE Publications.

Booth, D. (1994) *Story Drama: Reading, Writing and Role-Playing Across the Curriculum.* Markham, Ontario: Pembroke.

Bowell, P. & Heap, B. (2001) *Planning Process Drama.* London: David Fulton.

Burton, B. (1991) *The Act of Learning.* Melbourne: Longman Cheshire.

Burton, B. (1997) *Rehearsal for Life: Dramatising Adolescent Transitions through Recreational Youth Theatre.* Unpublished Doctoral Thesis, Department of Language and Literacy Education, Faculty of Education, University of Melbourne.

Burton, B., O'Toole, J. & Plunkett, A. (2005) From DRACON to Cooling Conflicts, in *DRACON International: Conflict Management and Drama* [working title]. UK: [publication under negotiation].

Byron, K. (1986) *Drama in the English Classroom.* London: Methuen.

Clifford, S. & Herrmann, A. (1999) *Making a Leap – Theatre of Empowerment*. London: Jessica Kingsley Publishers Ltd.

Cahill, H. (2002) Teaching for Community: Empowerment Through Drama. *Melbourne Studies in Education*, vol. 43, no. 2.

Cassidy, H. (2000) Using Drama to Relieve the Oppression of School Bullying. *Queensland Journal of Educational Research*, vol. 16, no. 2.

Cockett, S. (1998) What's 'Real' in Drama? *National Association for Drama in Education (Australia)*, 22 (2), pp. 33–43.

Donelan, K. (1999) Towards an Intercultural Aesthetic: 'The Gods Project' Biography. *NADIE Journal (Drama Australia Journal)*, 23 (2), pp. 65–80.

Dunn, J. (2000) *Dramatic Worlds in Play: A Study of the Changing Play of Pre-Adolescent Girls*. Unpublished Doctoral Dissertation, Faculty of Education, Griffith University, Brisbane.

Fyfe, H. (1996) Drama in the Context of a Divided Society, in J. O'Toole & K. Donelan (eds), *Drama, Culture and Empowerment: The IDEA Dialogues*, pp. 61–69. Brisbane: IDEA Publications.

Grady, S. (2000) *Drama and Diversity: A Pluralistic Perspective for Educational Drama*. Portsmouth, NH: Heinemann.

Heathcote, D. & Bolton, G. (1995) *Drama for Learning: Dorothy Heathcote's Mantle of the Expert Approach to Education*. Portsmouth, NH: Heinemann.

Johnson, L. & O'Neill, C. (eds) (1984) *Dorothy Heathcote: Collected Writings on Education and Drama*. London: Hutchinson.

Knezevic, D. (1995) Healing Power of Theatre, in P. Taylor and C. Hoepper (eds), *IDEA '95 Papers: Selected Readings in Drama and Theatre Education*. Brisbane: NADIE Publications, pp. 6–13.

McPhaill, I. (1984) Drama as a Paradigm of the Political Process, in D. Morton (ed.), *Drama for Capability*. Banbury, Oxon, UK: Kemble Press Ltd.

Morgan, N. & Saxton, J. (1987) *Teaching Drama*. Cheltenham, UK: Stanley Thornes Ltd.

Neelands, J. (1984) *Making Sense of Drama: A Guide to Classroom Practice*. Oxford, UK: Heinemann Educational Books Ltd.

O'Neill, C. (1994) Here Comes Everybody: Aspects of Role in Process Drama. *National Association for Drama in Education (Australia) Journal: International Research Issue*, 18 (2), pp. 37–44.

O'Neill, C. (1995) *Drama Worlds*. Portsmouth, NH: Heinemann.

O'Neill, C. (1996) Alienation and Empowerment, in J. O'Toole & K. Donelan (eds), *Drama, Culture and Empowerment: The IDEA Dialogues*, pp. 117–124. Brisbane: IDEA Publications.

O'Toole, J. (1992) *The Process of Drama*. London: Routledge.

O'Toole, J. (1995) The Rude Charms of Drama, in P. Taylor & C. Hoepper (eds), *IDEA '95: Selected Readings in Drama and Theatre Education*, pp. 78–87. Brisbane: NADIE Publications.

O'Toole, J. & Donelan, K. (1996) *Drama, Culture and Empowerment*. London: Routledge.

Pipkin, W. & Dimenna, S. (1989) Using Creative Dramatics to Teach Conflict Resolution: Exploiting the Drama/Conflict Dialectic. *The Journal of Humanistic Education and Development*, 28 (2), December, pp. 104–112.

Rimmington, K. (2002) Well, Bully to You Too! *Australian Drama Education Magazine* No. 7. Drama Australia.

Schonmann, S. (1996) The Drama and Theatre Class Battlefield, in J. O'Toole & K. Donelan (eds), *Drama, Culture and Empowerment: The IDEA Dialogues*, pp. 70–6. Brisbane: IDEA Publications.

Schutzman, M. & Cohen-Cruz, J. (eds) (1994) *Playing Boal: Theatre, Therapy, Activism*. London: Routledge, pp. 137–156.

Somers, J. (1994) *Drama in the Curriculum*. London: Cassell Educational Limited.

Taylor, P. (1998) *Redcoats & Patriots*. Portsmouth, NH: Heinemann.

Warner, C. (1995) *Exploring the Process of Engagement: An Examination of the Nature of Engagement in Drama When Used as a Methodology to Argument*. PhD Dissertation. UMI, ProQuest University Microfilms Inc. www.umi.com, Microform Number: 9534088.

Wilhelm, J. & Edmiston, B. (1998) *Imagining to Learn: Inquiry, Ethics and Integration through Drama*. Portsmouth, NH: Heinemann.

Wright, D. (1998) Embodied Learning: Approaching the Experience of the Body in Drama Education. *National Association for Drama in Education (Australia) Journal*, 22 (2), pp. 87–95.

Young, D. (2000) Reality Drama: The Drama Classroom as a Place for Disclosure. *NADIE Journal (Drama Australia Journal)*, 24 (1), pp. 111–22.

3. Peer teaching

Allen, V. (ed.) (1976) *Children as Teachers: Theory and Research on Tutoring*. New York: Academic Press.

Bagshaw, D. (1998) What Adolescents Say About Peer Mediation in Schools. Conference Proceedings, 4th National Mediation Conference, Mediation: Shaping the Future, in Tom Fisher (ed.), *Conference Proceedings*, La Trobe University, Melbourne, 4–8 April.

Billson, J. & Tiberius, R. (1991) Effective Social Arrangements for Teaching and Learning. *New Directions for Teaching and Learning*, no. 45, Spring.

Boyer, S. (1984) Peer Ears (Peer counselling program for high school students). *Children Today*, vol. 13, no. 3, pp. 21–24, July–August.

Briggs, D. (1998) *A Class of Their Own: When Children Teach Children.* Westport, CT: Bergin & Garvey.

Bruner, J. (1966) *Towards a Theory of Instruction.* Cambridge, MA: Harvard University.

Cram Donahue, M. (1996) How Does Peer Mediation Work? (Conflict resolution techniques; includes information about what makes a good mediator and how to start a peer mediation program). *Current Health* 2.

Dittmer, A. et al. (1993) Constructivist Teaching and Student Empowerment: Educational Equity through School Reform. *Equity and Excellence in Education*, vol. 26, no. 1, pp. 40–46, April.

Doneau, S. (1985) *What! Let Our Students Teach? Peer and Cross-Age Tutoring in Primary and Secondary Schools.* Sydney: Macquarie University.

Forsyth, I. (1999) *Delivering a Course: Practical Strategies for Teachers, Lecturers and Trainers.* London: Kogan Page.

Gabler, I. & Schroeder, M. (2003) *Seven Constructivist Methods for the Secondary Classroom – a planning guide for invisible teaching.* Boston, MA: Allyn & Bacon.

Goodlad, S. & Hirst, B. (1989) *Peer Tutoring: A Guide to Learning by Teaching.* London: Kogan Page.

Hensel, N.H. (1991) Leadership Giftedness: Social Leadership Skills in Young Children. *Roeper Review*, 14 (1), pp. 4–6, September.

Hopkins, D. (2002) *Improving the Quality of Education for All.* London: David Fulton.

Kantrowitz, B. (1993) The Group Classroom: Why Team Learning May Finally Be Catching On (cooperative learning in high school). *Newsweek*, vol. 121, no. 19, p. 73, May.

Koch, M. & Miller, S. (1987) Resolving Student Conflicts with Student Mediators. *Principal*, 66, pp. 59–61.

Kowalski, K. (1998) Peer Mediation Success Stories: In Nearly 10,000 Schools Nationwide, Peer Mediation Helped Teens Solve Problems without Violence. *Current Health* 2, vol. 25, no. 2, pp. 13–16, October.

Melaragno, R. (1976) The Tutorial Community, in V.L. Allen (ed.), *Children as Teachers: Theory and Research on Tutoring*, pp. 189–198. New York: Academic Press.

Morrison, M. (2004) Risk and Responsibility: The Potential of Peer Teaching to Address Negative Leadership. Cambridge, UK: unpublished article.

Powell, K. et al. (1995) A Review of Selected School-Based Conflict Resolution and Peer Mediation Projects. *Journal of School Health*, vol. 65, no. 10, pp. 426–432, December.

Robbins, P. (1991) *How to Plan and Implement a Peer-Coaching Program.* Richmond, VA: Association for Supervision & Curriculum Development.

Rubin, J. & Herbert, M. (1998) Peer Teaching – Model for Active Learning. *College Teaching*, Winter, vol. 48, no. 1.

Simmons, D. et al. (1995) Effects of Explicit Teaching and Peer Tutoring on the Reading Achievement of Learning-Disabled and Low-Performing Students in Regular Classrooms. *The Elementary School Journal*, vol. 95, no. 5.

Stomfay-Stitz, A. (1994) Conflict Resolution and Peer Mediation: Pathways to Safer Schools (creating safer environments for children in the home, school and community). *Childhood Education Annual*, vol. 70, no. 5, pp. 279–283.

Svinicki, M. (1991) Practical Implications of Cognitive Theories. *New Directions for Teaching and Learning*, no. 45, p. 30.

Townley, A. (1995) Changing School Culture (conflict resolution through peer mediation). *Educational Leadership*, vol. 52, no. 8, p. 80, May.

Vygotsky, L. (1976) Play and its Role in the Mental Development of the Child, in J. Bruner, A. Jolly & K. Silva (eds), *Play: Its Role in Development and Evolution*. New York: Basic Books, pp. 537–554.

Wagner, L. (1982) *Peer Teaching: Historical Perspectives*. London: Greenwood Press.